The Franco-Prussian War: The History of the War that Established the German Empire

By Charles River Editors

A painting depicting the surrender of Emperor Napoleon III during the war

About Charles River Editors

Charles River Editors provides superior editing and original writing services across the digital publishing industry, with the expertise to create digital content for publishers across a vast range of subject matter. In addition to providing original digital content for third party publishers, we also republish civilization's greatest literary works, bringing them to new generations of readers via ebooks.

Sign up here to receive updates about free books as we publish them, **and visit** Our Kindle Author Page to browse today's free promotions and our most recently published Kindle titles.

Introduction

A painting depicting Wilhelm I's coronation as emperor

The Franco-Prussian War

Locked in a balance of power since the 1815 Congress of Vienna, the world was dominated by the great European powers of Britain, France, Russia, and Austria, and at the Congress of Vienna itself, Prussia had been a minor concern. Though the Prussians had come through in time to assist the Duke of Wellington at Waterloo, they were nevertheless taken for granted at the conference, with the major powers instead preferring to deal with the more historically powerful Austrian Hapsburgs. In his scathing commentary on Prussian culture, *When Blood is Their Argument*, Ford Maddox Ford attempted to explain the sudden rise of Prussian political and economic status from 1849–1880, writing, "She [Prussia] had pushed herself from being a bad second in the comity of Germanism into a position of equality with, if not of predominance over, Austria, amongst the German peoples."[1]

Prussian leaders, especially Otto von Bismarck, the chancellor and advisor to Prussia's king, believed Prussia could be a united and respected power, but only without the traditional Austrian

---

[1] Ford Maddox Ford, When Blood Is Their Argument: An Analysis of Prussian Culture (London: Hodder and Stoughton, 1915), 82.

dominance. At the time, the Austrian empire was a collection of ethnically diverse peoples and had been dominated by a socio-political conservatism that sought to keep the empire ruled in Hapsburg tradition.

After Prussia was victorious in the Austro-Prussian War, Bismarck played a waiting game where the unification of Germany was concerned, as the joining of the southern states - initially resistant to Prussian rule, friendly with Austria, and bent on independence - would have to be overcome. What was needed was "a clear case of French aggression"[2] toward either Prussia or the southern states. Not only would such a move by Emperor Napoleon III trigger the terms of the treaty between the German states, but it would keep the remaining world powers out of the conflict.[3]

It would be a dispute over the throne of Spain that would cause Napoleon III to act. During a revolution, Queen of Spain Isabella was forced to flee Madrid. Spain was divided over who would rule, and the other European nations had a decided interest in the matter. In the months that followed, Prince Leopold of Hohenzollern was suggested as a fitting heir. His name, as well as many others, circulated amongst the powerful and the influential. Some have suggested Bismarck had orchestrated the naming of Leopold as successor to tie Spain to Germany, but most historians dispute his direct involvement in the matter. Leopold's attractions included the fact that he was "the husband of a Portuguese princess, related both to the royal house of Prussia and to Napoleon III, and with several sons to carry on the line."[4] Though many candidates were considered - including Leopold's younger brother, Charles, who was a ruling Romanian prince - they were deemed unacceptable to some party of influence in heavily fractious Spain, unacceptable to hold such a great power, or they were uninterested.

The impertinence of the French toward the Prussian king, the Hohenzollerns, and their presumption of right in the matter quickly turned public opinion against the French in Prussia. Bismarck fanned the flames by taking an offended tone. "It was impossible that Prussia could tamely and quietly sit under the affront offered to the king and to the nation by the menacing language of the French government," he said.

Believing France had prepared for success in a quick war against the Prussians, Napoleon III took the bait and declared war against Prussia on July 19, 1870.[5] The French declared war as much against Bismarck as they had against Prussia, believing he had manipulated the Spanish ascendancy in an effort to seek power, rather than peace.

The Franco-Prussian War started in August 1870, and a number of victories followed for the

---

[2] Ibid., 67.
[3] Ibid.
[4] Lawrence D. Steefel, Bismarck, the Hohenzollern Candidacy, and the Origins of the Franco-German War of 1870 (Cambridge, MA: Harvard University Press, 1962), 22.
[5] George O. Kent, 71.

Prussians in battles in northeast France. By September, the strategic city of Metz was under siege, and forces fought a major battle at Sedan. Led by Field Marshal Helmuth von Moltke, the Prussians forced the French to surrender at Metz, and then at Sedan. Emperor Napoleon III, commanding his country's forces at Sedan, was taken prisoner, humiliating France and its impetuous leader.

The Prussians immediately marched on Paris, but the capital refused to submit, and a separate siege was mounted that ended up lasting 130 days. Obviously, French society was in tumult, but a Third Republic and Government of National Defence was pronounced in place of the French Empire. An uprising subsequently took place in the stricken city, dubbed the "Paris Commune," which sought to establish a radical alternative to the status quo and was itself put down by French troops.[6]

Prussian forces besieged Paris starting in September 1870, and although French units attempted to make inroads at battles in the north and east of the country, the Prussians were in comfortable control of the conflict. Food was becoming scarce, and an armistice was signed on January 26, 1871 with Paris on the brink of starvation. The Prussians lost 45,000 men during the conflict, while France suffered almost three times as many dead and wounded. The French government accepted the terms of its defeat with the Germans, which would prove a painful experience, and for their part, the Prussians could avenge the humiliation of the Napoleonic occupation and the treatment at the hands of the French conqueror 65 years earlier.

To Napoleon, defeat meant territorial annexation and financial reparations, and the same treatment was now to be meted out in reverse. France was forced to recognize the new German Empire and pay five billion francs in reparations, the exact equivalent of what Napoleon had levied in 1807.

A peace treaty was signed, the Treaty of Frankfurt, on May 10, 1871, and as a part of the treaty, Prussia annexed the predominantly German-speaking region of Alsace-Lorraine (known as Elsass-Lothringen in German), including Strasbourg, the ancient center of the region.[7] The German Army returned to Berlin and marched triumphantly (and with historical symbolism) through the Brandenburg Gate on June 16, 1871, marking Prussia's complete recovery from its lowest point in 1806.[8]

On January 18, 1871, King Wilhelm I was crowned Kaiser of the German Empire, and though the Franco-Prussian War was still taking place, this moment was essentially the point at which

[6] Alistair Horne, *The Fall of Paris: The Siege and the Commune 1870-71*, (London: Penguin, 2007)

[7] German Historical Institute, 'August Bebel Criticizes the Franco-Prussian War and the Annexation of Alsace-Lorraine in a Speech before the North German Reichstag (November 26, 1870)', http://germanhistorydocs.ghi-dc.org/sub_document.cfm?document_id=673, [accessed 6 August 2018]

[8] *Deutsche Welle*, 'The Germans – Bismarck', 17 June 2018, https://www.dw.com/en/the-germans-bismarck/av-44261040, [accessed 7 August 2018]

Germany was unified. The other German states had to agree to this profound constitutional change, but they acquiesced after the clear victory of the Prussian-led forces. German unification was the territorial expansion of Prussia by another name, but Berlin demonstrated it could protect the interests, or at least the safety, of German-speakers under their watch.

Despite the campaigns of nationalists and liberals over the previous decades, it was ultimately a victory on the battlefield that united the German states. This was the real-world application of Bismarck's "Blood and Iron" concept. From this position of strength during war, Prussia achieved an unassailable position. During the relatively short wars of 1864, 1866, and 1870-71, Bismarck roused nationalist sentiment, and in so doing, he achieved the long awaited goal of German unification. Nevertheless, the manner in which Germany was united drew much criticism. Prussia was at the head of a militarized state led by an authoritarian regime. This version of a German Reich would move irrevocably toward the First World War, which started 43 years after the Empire's founding. For many, nationalism became a substitute for political participation in the unified Germany.[9]

The Franco-Prussian War: The History of the War that Established the German Empire looks at the important conflict and its geopolitical ramifications. Along with pictures of important people, places, and events, you will learn about the Franco-Prussian War like never before.

---

[9] Richard Evans, *Rereading German History: From Unification to Reunification 1800-1996* (Routledge, 1997), p. 46.

The Congress of Vienna

The history of Germany and the German-speaking peoples is as complex and multifaceted as any in Europe. It is also one of the most difficult to pinpoint conceptually and historically, since every nation is a construct to some extent. Language is certainly important, and the German language is a unifying factor for any notion of a unified Germany, yet even today, many German-speakers live outside the borders of modern Germany. Shared customs and traditions gave Germans a common sense of identity to some extent, but these were often local in origin. Germans were also split between several versions of Christianity.

Nevertheless, ideas of a German nation were present by the 19th century, leading up to the official unification in 1871. Neil MacGregor, a historian of modern Germany, has explained that the two defining events leading to the rise of German nationalism and the movement toward unification were the Thirty Years' War and the Napoleonic Wars.[10] During the Thirty Years' War, more than 200 German states were part of the Holy Roman Empire's loose confederation, and that war was predominantly fought in German states by foreign powers, including France, Sweden, Denmark, Austria, and the Netherlands. MacGregor noted that "horrors were experienced across all Germany, and were never forgotten," to the extent that they were invoked during World War II.[11] The religious basis of the Thirty Years' War saw the split between Catholicism and Protestantism, which was at the heart of the Reformation. Some foreign leaders even invoked defending "German freedoms" for their invasion.[12]

From the German point of view, the Thirty Years' War was proof of their vulnerability to foreign aggression. Atrocities such as the "sacking" of Magdeburg in 1631, where more than 30,000 people were killed, were embedded in the German consciousness.[13] All told, 8 million people died during the Thirty Years' War.

Likewise, the Napoleonic Wars, fought about 150 years later, appeared to confirm these fears. The French Revolution had terrified similar royal regimes in other European empires, and as the revolution took on ever bloodier connotations, other countries were drawn into conflict with the new French Republic, with the Holy Roman Empire on the front line of the revolutionary wars. Napoleon Bonaparte earned his reputation with a number of victories on the battlefield and rose to the pinnacle of power in France. As the French emperor, his reign was characterized by a more aggressive military strategy and the rapid annexation of much of Europe.

---

[10] Neil MacGregor, *Germany: Memories of a Nation* (London: Penguin, 2016), p. xviii
[11] Ibid.
[12] Brendan Simms, *Europe: The Struggle for Supremacy 1453 to the Present* (London: Penguin, 2014), pp. 39-40.
[13] German Historical Institute, 'Volume 1: From the Reformation to the Thirty Years War, 1500-1648
A Local Apocalypse – The Sack of Magdeburg (1631)', http://germanhistorydocs.ghi-dc.org/pdf/eng/85.SackMagdeburg_en.pdf, [accessed 6 August 2018]

Napoleon

The Rhineland was occupied even in the 1790s, and 1806, even Prussia, the largest German state, had been defeated. Prussia had been founded in 1701 out of the state of Brandenburg and extended its power and territory over the following century under the reign of Frederick the Great.[14] In 1806, however, the Prussian monarchy was forced into a humiliating retreat and exile, while Napoleon rode through the recently built Brandenburg Gate in Berlin. This would not be forgotten by the German people. The French ruler annexed German lands, dissolved the Holy Roman Empire, and forced Prussia to pay war reparations, and this pattern of military victory, annexation, and reparations would affect relations between the two sides over the next 100 years.[15]

---

[14] Known as Friedrich der Große in German.
[15] Neil MacGregor, *Germany: Memories of a Nation* (London: Penguin, 2016), p. 256.

Frederick the Great

One of Napoleon's first steps after the demise of the Holy Roman Empire was to set up the Confederation of the Rhine in 1806, which was essentially a puppet regime in the German states stretching from Bavaria in the south to the Baltic Sea. This would remain occupied until 1813, when the French went into retreat after the Battle of Leipzig. Prussia mounted a campaign to retake its territory after Napoleon's defeat in Russia, and Leipzig, the biggest battle of the Napoleonic Wars in terms of numbers, was one of the key battles in this comeback. As a means of mobilizing its population, the Prussian leadership introduced a number of social reforms, including widening access to education. At the same time, Prussia made military service compulsory, which undoubtedly assisted in the French's eventual defeat. It also had the effect of militarizing Prussian politics and society, a point the state's critics would continue to shed light on, even during the rise of the Nazis.

The Prussians, in coalition with several other countries and forces, finally defeated Napoleon in 1815 at Waterloo, and the subsequent Congress of Vienna would cement its place as leader of the German-speaking states and a major European power. By then, the French occupation, as well as the memory of the Thirty Years' War, had cultivated a sense of solidarity amongst German speakers, despite their many geographical and cultural differences. Many had volunteered to fight Napoleon's armies during the conflicts through a feeling of camaraderie. The occupation accelerated a sense of "German-ness," and German-speaking composers such as Wolfgang Amadeus Mozart and Ludwig van Beethoven were co-opted to form a sense of cultural excellence and civilization along with the formalization of the German language, which increased as the 19th century progressed. Other German writers, painters, and composers emphasized traditions, which helped construct a national "story". The Brothers Grimm, for instance, were born in Hessen in the time of the Holy Roman Empire, and it is perhaps no coincidence they published their first volume of fairy tales in 1812, a year before the end of the Confederation of the Rhine.[16] The Brothers Grimm specialized in German folklore, invoking rural and sometimes graphic themes, which became omnipotent across German-speaking territories. *Little Red Riding Hood*, *The Pied Piper of Hamelin*, and *Rumpelstiltskin* became children's staples and helped construct a national "hinterland."[17]

The Congress of Vienna, which took place over several months during 1814 and 1815, was an attempt to resolve the numerous challenges presented by Napoleon's expansion and his subsequent defeat. The talks have been seen as a critical moment in European history, and depending on the point-of-view, the results were either a diplomatic breakthrough or the last gasps of the continent's conservative elites. It was also a crucial step toward German unification, although this was not clear at the time.

French expansionism had put Europe in a state of flux. The coalition forces that ultimately defeated Napoleon were a combination of the Austrian Habsburgs, Russia, Prussia, and the British, all of whom wanted to impose terms on France at Vienna to mold the continent in their interests. Vienna was chosen as one of the victorious powers and the home for a huge central and southeastern European empire, and the key actors at Vienna were Austrian Foreign Minister Count Klemens von Metternich and British Foreign Minister Lord Castlereagh. Their ultimate aims were to secure or impose a balance of power in Europe according to new geopolitical realities.

---

[16] Neil MacGregor, *Germany: Memories of a Nation* (London: Penguin, 2016), p. 114.
[17] Joan Acocella, 'Once Upon a Time: The lure of the Fairy Tale', *The New Yorker*, 23 July 2012, https://www.newyorker.com/magazine/2012/07/23/once-upon-a-time-3, [accessed 6 August 2018]

Metternich

Castlereagh

Leaders in 1814-1815 were broadly opposed to both republicanism and revolution, and the outcome of the Congress reflected these principles. One of the key features of Vienna was, therefore, the re-ordering of German states into a German Confederation, or *Deutscher Bund*.[18] The Confederation was, in essence, a re-imagining of the Holy Roman Empire, but with 39 states. Prussia's role was recognized, and it was granted new territory in the Rhineland, including the large city of Cologne.[19] Crucially, the Austrians were to head the new, albeit loose Confederation.

Even as this took place, Metternich was deeply conservative and fearful of liberalism and nationalism's impact within the German states, particularly concerning Prussia's potential leadership role. The new arrangement would, therefore, attempt to contain German nationalism. Metternich and Castlereagh also constructed the so-called "Concert of Europe", whereby leading European powers would engage in regular diplomacy to resolve future challenges. This system developed during the 19th century, and although it was flawed, it managed to prevent major military conflagrations.

Of course, despite the fact the Vienna settlement limited new political forces such as nationalism, it could not subsequently prevent them from reappearing with even more potency. Nonetheless, the Concert of Europe model would reappear in the form of the League of Nations and then the United Nations after further disastrous wars, ones that involved Germany more directly.

The Austro-Prussian War

Bismarck, as the prime minister of Prussia, has been credited with Prussia's rise and eventual German unity, but also excoriated for laying the foundation for modern fascism in Germany. His diplomatic manipulation is recognized by those on both sides of the argument; he is always described, whether positively or negatively, as a man willing to do whatever was necessary to accomplish his goals. For Ford, Bismarck was "the greatest opportunist in the history of the world."[20] Rejecting the idea that Bismarck was simply the right Prussian at the right time for Prussian ascendance, Ford countered, "Prussia was being pulled forward by one single man, who, as we shall see later, gasped and staggered and clutched at twigs which broke, and gave ground and cried with nervous exhaustion when he himself had reduced the King of Prussia to tears of an exhaustion equally nervous."[21] Bismarck had determined that Austrian status must decline if Prussia was to elevate its status as a world power.[22]

---

[18] Brendan Simms, *Europe: The Struggle for Supremacy 1453 to the Present* (London: Penguin, 2014), p. 182.
[19] Michael Rowe, 'France, Prussia, or Germany? The Napoleonic Wars and Shifting Allegiances in the Rhineland', *Central European History*, (39:4, Dec 2006, pp. 611-640), pp. 611-612.
[20] Ford Maddox Ford, 81.
[21] Ibid.
[22] Van Evera, Stephen. "The Austro-Prussian War of 1866." Causes and Prevention of War, Massachusetts Institute of Technology, Cambridge, Massachusetts, Spring 2009.

Bismarck in 1863

The Prussians, upstarts from the beginning, had desired such change for decades, but "most of Bismarck's predecessors thought in terms of a political rather than a military humiliation of Austria…In his attitude to foreign policy Bismarck differed from them in two important respects: he was prepared to carry the process of the revision of the 1815 settlement in Germany farther than they had ever contemplated, and he was also willing to exploit any opportunity to achieve his ends."[23]

After the demise of Napoleon, however, one power could not act without the approval or at least neutrality of the others, so regardless of whether one agrees with Ford's "one single man" view of Bismarck or not, Bismarck had to face certain realities. Put simply, Russia, France, Britain, and even Italy would have to be convinced that Prussia's actions against Austria would benefit them, or at the very least that the balance of power would not be affected. Bismarck would set out to do just that, and to move so quickly that there would hardly be time for

---

[23] F. R. Bridge and Roger Bullen, The Great Powers and the European States System, 1815-1914 (London: Longman, 1980), 97.

international reaction, but as it turned out, Russia, Britain, and to a lesser extent France all convinced themselves of it anyway. Bismarck's relationship with key players in the Russian government allowed the Russians to believe that their common interests would be strengthened by Prussian ascendance. The British, aiming to steer clear of European continental conflicts, were more concerned with the French than the Austrians, and France believed Prussia and Austria were so closely matched that the French would be needed to break the stalemate and receive a just reward.

At the same time, Italy was primed for conflict with Austria and, because of its history, could be easily convinced to ally with the Prussians in exchange for promises of land and revenge against the Austrians. Despite growing nationalism in Italy, in 1866 it remained divided, and it was not until 1870 that Italy was a united and modern nation-state. In 1815, Austria, with the approval of the great powers, helped itself to the rich Italian provinces of Lombardy and Venetia, and from that time until 1859, Austria acted as Italy's "gendarme," in the words of Geoffrey Wawro. When Italian nationalists rose against the "restored regimes in Piedmont, Rome, Naples, and the Italian duchies," Austria made sure "to crush opposition," sending in troops in 1815, 1821, 1830, 1831, and 1847.[24]

With no love lost between the Italians and Austria, the Italians were a ready ally for Prussia if convinced that a military alliance would give them the diplomatic and military respect they craved. For their part, the Prussians and General Helmuth von Moltke the Elder believed that the Italian army was necessary for Prussian success in any conflict against the Austrians. Threats from Italian forces would preoccupy the Austrians, allowing Prussia to put its armies into solid strategic positions.[25]

---

[24] Geoffrey Wawro, *The Austro-Prussian War: Austria's War with Prussia and Italy in 1866.* (New York: Cambridge University Press, 1996), 47.

[25] George O. Kent, 54.

Helmuth von Moltke the Elder

Of course, the German people also needed convincing. After many years of relative peace with the European powers, "most governments claimed at the outset of wars that they were the innocent victims of aggression and urged the people to unite in defense of their fatherland. Governments felt it necessary to conceal their very specific territorial ambitions behind general and idealized value. In 1866 Bismarck asked Germans to fight Germans, not for Prussian expansion, but for the sake of the fatherland."[26] This Germanic nationalism would eventually carry Bismarck to war against the French as well, creating the first German nation-state in 1871, but for now, "Germany" was just an idea. Instead, a strong Prussian kingdom was the potential leader for Germanic people seeking unity without Austrian involvement.

In his commentary on the military significance of the Battle of Königgrätz, American General Arthur Wagner provided a timeline of events leading to the outbreak of war between Austria and Prussia. Tellingly, Wagner's timeline begins with the Treaty of Vienna in October of 1864, and for a proper understanding of what led to the Austro-Prussian conflict, it is necessary to understand the recent actions of an allied Austro-Prussia union in the matter of Denmark.

At the time, "Germany" was far more conceptual than a political or geographical reality. The

---

[26] F. R. Bridge and Roger Bullen, *The Great Powers and the European States System*, 1815-1914 (London: Longman, 1980), 83.

German Confederation, established in 1815 as a result of the defeat of Napoleon, included 39 separate German states, each with their own history and political leanings. For many Germans, the idea of unity was attractive, but while some dreamed of a Germany united under Austria's leadership (a vision known as *Grossdeutschland*), others preferred to exclude the Austrians and looked instead to Prussia (*Kleindeutschland*).[27] Prussia and Austria competed for leadership in Germany, especially as Prussia strengthened its military and economic powers and Austria weakened in the face of internal conflicts. The appointment of Bismarck to the Frankfurt Diet in 1851, and later to the position of Prussian Chief Minister in 1862, would prove crucial to how the question of German unity would be answered.

Despite the underlying conflict, Prussia and Austria had united in the fight against the King of Denmark in 1864. King Christian IX, new to the throne, attempted to abrogate the London Protocol, an earlier agreement by the now-deceased Frederick VII that had promised continuing independence for the duchies of Schleswig and Holstein. Danish domination of these German-speaking areas represented an affront to those who dreamed of unity, whether Austrian or Prussian led.

Christian IX

Both Austria and Prussia had significant reasons for opposing the Danish King. For Austria,

[27] Feuchtwanger, Edgar. "Bismarck, Prussia & German Nationalism," *History Review*, 2001.

any ethnic division, such as the Danish-German split in Holstein, represented a threat to its multiethnic empire, a heterogeneous aggregation of Germans, Czechs, Magyars, Poles, Croats and Italians bound together in a purely artificial nationality.[28] Already plagued by divisions in the east with the Hungarian Magyars, Austria wanted to maintain the status quo in the duchies.

Prussia, and particularly Bismarck, on the other hand, had more pragmatic reasons for opposing Danish rule. Bismarck had designs on the port of Kiel in Schleswig, and if the new Danish king appeared to violate the promises of the past, European opinion might allow a "defensive" attack by Prussian troops that would allow the taking of the port. At the same time, if Prussia sent troops there, Austria could not merely stand by and risk the appearance of Prussian leadership in an international matter. Thus, in February of 1864, without opposition from England, France, or Russia, the Austrians and Prussians began an "execution" against the actions of the Danes, sending troops representing the federal Diet of the German Confederation into Schleswig.[29] The war, fought over limited goals and local border disputes, rather than international causes, can be categorized as a cabinet war (*Kabinetskriege*), or as military historian John Broom put it, "clearly a cabinet war."[30]

The war's result brought no independence to the people of either Schleswig or Holstein, but simply placed them squarely under the dominion of Austria and Prussia, a condominium ruled jointly.[31] Though the Treaty of Vienna promised "future peace and friendship between their Majesties the King of Prussia and the Emperor of Austria and his Majesty the King of Denmark as well as between their heirs and successors, their respective states and subjects in perpetuity,"[32] nothing could have been further from the truth.

Bismarck had known that relations between the Prussians and Austrians were fraught with difficulty. The countries were uneasy allies against Denmark, and Bismarck subsequently proceeded with what he believed was necessary to accomplish his goals for Prussia, which had meant an alliance with Austria in 1864. To a critic of his policy, Bismarck replied, "You do not trust Austria. Nor do I; but I think it right to have Austria with us now; we shall see later whether the moment of parting comes and from whom."[33]

Almost immediately after the Danish War, Austria and Prussia were at odds over the rule of the former duchies. Bismarck, of course, wanted these northern duchies for Prussia, a stance Austria firmly opposed. Austria, listening to the cries of the southern states of the German confederation, believed it was justified in demanding that the duchies remain independent from any nation, but

[28] Arthur Wagner, 6.

[29] Martin Kitchen, A History of Modern Germany, 1800 to the Present, 2nd ed. (Malden, MA: Wiley-Blackwell, 2012), 97.

[30] John T. Broom.

[31] Ibid., 98.

[32] Augustus Oakes and R. B. Mowat, eds. *The Great European Treaties of the Nineteenth Century*. Oxford: (Clarendon Press, 1918), 199.

[33] A. J. P. Taylor, Bismarck: The Man and the Statesman (New York: Vintage Books, 1967), 74

jointly ruled by the Duke of Augustenberg, a claimant to the throne.[34]

Historians debate Bismarck's motives here; had he simply wanted to rule the new territories as a plan to strengthen Prussia itself or was his insistence at controlling Schleswig-Holstein part of a plan to draw Austria into a conflict?[35] *The New York Times* reported on "The Schleswig-Holstein Question" in June of 1865, calling the escalating tension between Austria and Prussia "entertaining":

> "Each of these powers entered into the war against Denmark with the full intention of cheating each other, and pocketing the lion's share of the spoils…no sane man out of Germany ever believed that the crusade against the little mother kingdom was begun for the purpose of delivering the Schleswig-Holsteiners from Danish rule. Everybody knew that Prussia had an eye on Kiel, as a commodious harbor for her prospective navy. Austria wanted another ally among the small German States that support her against Prussia, and assist in checkmating the ambitious designs of king WILHELM and Herr BISMARCK…the people at large supported the war from a vague notion that it might lead to grand results in the way of German unity, that unfulfilled dream of many centuries…with the conclusion of peace came bitter jealousies, accusations and recriminations, that threaten to set all Germany together by the ears. Prussia, having the most to gain, made the first dash for the spoils. She seized upon the important seaport of Kiel, and commenced there the erection of fortifications and dockyards, with the aid of a person that felt entirely at home and meant to stay. When Austria remonstrated, Count BISMARCK serenely smiled, and uttered a few "glittering generalities" about the glory of Prussia being inseparably entwined with that of all the German States…Like a prudent statesman, he is content to move slowly, occasionally throwing a little dust in his adversary's eyes. He still keeps up a show of negotiation with Austria and the Federal Diet, and even proposes to allow the people of Schleswig-Holstein to express their sentiments through on election, which he well knows will do them no possible good, nor stand in the way of the accomplishment of his own designs."[36]

In August 1865, Austria was forced to agree to the convention of Gastein, which allowed Prussia to rule Schleswig while Austria ruled Holstein.[37] This left the Austrian government in the position of pleasing very few, as Austrian and southern German supporters of the Augustenberg candidacy felt he had been betrayed. Indeed, those who opposed the rise of Prussia felt like victims of a "Bismarckian trap". The German General Staff later called the

---

[34] Ibid., 97.
[35] Ibid.
[36] "Prussia and Austria: The Schleswig Holstein Question." *The New York Times*, June 11, 1865.
[37] "Convention of Gastein." Encyclopaedia Britannica, s.v. "Internet." Chicago: Encyclopaedia Britannica, 2016.

administration of the duchies by both countries a "momentary understanding…only a postponement, not a definite settlement, of the question at issue."[38]

Tensions rose between Austria and Prussia as "the less security Prussia found in the German Confederation, the more was she compelled to seek for an ally elsewhere."[39] Other nations were understandably tempted to choose sides. The Italians, not yet united but desiring a national cause that could bring them together, along with giving them a claim to territory taken by Austria, promised Prussia an alliance in any conflict with Austria. The condition under which the promise was granted was that any conflict in which the Italians would aid Prussia must take place within three months. This timeline put pressure on Bismarck to act, but he also had to make sure Prussia didn't appear to be the non-aggressor. France, in turn, promised Austria neutrality but not aid in a war involving the Prussians.[40]

Continuing disagreements over the state of the duchies eventually compelled Austria to ask for a decision from the Diet at Frankfurt. The Diet was the legislative body of the German Confederation, but it had been dominated by Austria's representatives for years. In asking the confederation to decide the question, rather than continuing to deal with Prussia as an ally in the matter of the duchies, the Austrians "had made the first open gesture of hostility."[41]

Prussia responded by marching troops into Holstein,[42] and with that, Bismarck seized the opportunity to challenge traditional Austrian dominance while appearing only to defend Prussia's interests. There would be weeks of negotiations and diplomacy before the Austro-Prussian War began, but in *The Great Powers and the European States System, 1815-1914*, authors F.R. Bridge and Roger Bullen claim that from May 1866 on, both powers "accepted that war between them was inevitable."[43] The authors even claim that Bismarck used backchannels to offer the Austrians a way out of the conflict, with roughly the same moderate terms he planned to bring to the table after Austria's defeat.[44]

That summer, most of Europe put more stock in the armies of Austria. Since the Prussians had not been tested in a major conflict since Waterloo in 1815, many believed that the "Sparta of the north" was past its prime, and though Austria had been defeated by the Italians in the Battle of Solferino, the Austrians had recent combat experience, superiority of numbers, and a longer history. With that said, and with the advantage of hindsight, military historian Arthur Wagner noted the disparity between appearances and reality at the start of the war - though Austria was twice as large as Prussia with a population advantage of 15 million, the Prussians had the

[38] Generalstab Grosser, 2.

[39] Ibid., 8.

[40] Martin Kitchen, 99.

[41] A. J. P. Taylor, Bismarck: The Man and the Statesman (New York: Vintage Books, 1967), 83.

[42] George O. Kent, Bismarck and His Times (Carbondale, IL: Southern Illinois University Press, 1978), 59.

[43] F. R. Bridge and Roger Bullen, The Great Powers and the European States System, 1815-1914 (London: Longman, 1980), 104.

[44] Ibid.

advantage.[45]

As the war began, the smaller German states had to choose sides. Those siding with Prussia included "Saxe-Coburg-Gotha, Lippe, Oldenburg, [and] Hansetowns."[46] This added about 28,000 men, in addition to the Prussian forces and the 200,000 Italians pledged to assist Prussia. Prussia had about 720,000 men under arms between the regular army and the Landwehr, which was the home defense created by the requirement for all men to serve.[47] The Landwehr required that previously trained soldiers remain in inactive service for 11 years, and its strength lay in its organization. "In peace everything is always kept ready for the mobilization of the army, every officer and every official knows during peace what will be his post and what will be his duty the moment the decree for the mobilization is issued, and the moment that decree is flashed by telegraph to the most distant stations everyone sets about his necessary duty without requiring any further orders or any explanations."[48] As such, Prussia had not only great leadership but men at the ready and a mobilization plan activated by the most modern communication and transportation systems in continental Europe.

Austria had an army of 600,000[49] and was supported by most of the German states (which sided with Austria in the final vote of the German Diet on June 12, 1866[50]), totaling 141,000 men. However, despite the huge advantages in population and men under arms, the issue of mobilization was key. Like Russia at the start of World War I, Austria's need for an extended time to get the military in place and ready to fight would prove an obstacle. The necessity to announce mobilization also limited Austria's diplomatic options. The German General Staff report, published in 1878, charges Austria with a clear breach of its own claims to desire peace due simply to the mobilization efforts in the spring of 1866. For the writer of that report, the freedom of the Prussian press and the organization of the Prussian army made deception impossible on the Prussian side. Austria, he argued, was the aggressor because the Austrians "overrode the stipulations of the Conventions of Vienna and Gastein" by moving troops, repairing military fortresses, purchasing horses, and calling up men in reserve.[51] Prussia, in his view, had delayed its mobilization, which was necessarily the equivalent of war footing, though "for even in May the hope that hostilities might still with honour be avoided had not been entirely abandoned."[52] Instead, Prussia was forced to respond to Austrian aggression with its own mobilization.

[45] Arthur Wagner, 6.
[46] J.H. Anderson, *The Austro-Prussian War in Bohemia, 1866: Otherwise known as the Seven Weeks' War or Needle-Gun War.* (London: Hugh Rees, Ltd., 1908), 17.
[47] Ibid., 19.
[48] Henry Hozier, 65.
[49] J.H. Anderson, 19.
[50] F. R. Bridge and Roger Bullen, The Great Powers and the European States System, 1815-1914 (London: Longman, 1980), 104.
[51] General
[52] General Grosser, 11.

Just 10 weeks after the outbreak of war, the Treaty of Prague was signed on August 23, 1866. Though the war itself was a contained fight between two powers, the Austro-Prussian conflict resulted in a "territorial and political settlement of 1866-67 in central Europe [that] was the single most important and extensive revision of the treaties of 1815. The Prussian annexations in Germany made her larger, more populous and richer than all the other German states combined. Austria ceased at one blow to be an Italian and German power, relinquishing Venetia to France (who transferred it to Italy) at the same time as she was expelled from Germany. The loose Confederation of 1815 was replaced by the new centrally-controlled and Prussian-dominated Confederation of 1867.... Short localized wars between two powers had, as one British diplomat observed, replaced conference diplomacy of all the powers as the principal means of treaty revision. The 1815 settlement in central Europe was totally destroyed."[53]

In the immediate aftermath of the Austro-Prussian victory, Bismarck enjoyed political favor, if not a consolidated base of support, as the Prussian mood seemed to have swung in the direction of the pragmatic: "Prussia's victory of 1866 seemed to convince many of the advantages of the realpolitik of the 1860s over the idealism of the 1840s. People wearied of supporting the unsuccessful policies of Austria and were frustrated by the seemingly unattainable goals of liberalism and constitutionalism. But beyond that, the unification of the country under Prussian leadership now seemed within reach."[54] Bismarck believed a new Northern German Confederation was a political necessity, but the unification of the south and the formation of Germany as a nation would have to wait.

Bismarck was undoubtedly one of the most important politicians of the 19th century, but for most historians, it was Prussia's military and economic superiority, not Bismarck's leadership, that should be credited for the victory over the Austrians. Its railroads and communication lines, its ability to lean on trained conscripts in reserve, and its superior weaponry in the breech-loading needle gun all led to a Prussian victory in only seven weeks of war.[55]

Napoleon III and France in 1870

France struggled to assert itself against the British, Austrians, and Russians after the defeat at Waterloo 1815, and with their victory in the Austro-Prussian War, the Prussians added to France's troubles as a potential challenger to the east. The Prussian victory had come as a surprise to French Emperor Napoleon III.

---

[53] F. R. Bridge and Roger Bullen, 105.
[54] George O. Kent, 62.
[55] Robert Pearce, "The Austro-Prussian War: Robert Pearce Examines the Factors That Led to Prussia's Victory in the German Civil War of 1866," *History Review*, no. 66 (2010).

Napoleon III

   Born as the third son of Napoleon Bonaparte's brother, Louis, and his wife, Hortense, Louis Napoleon had a remote chance of inheriting the empire from his uncle. Not only was he fourth in line, but the empire had collapsed in 1815 upon his uncle's final exile. After the restoration of the Bourbons, another revolution, and the establishment of a constitutional king in Louis Phillipe, Louis Napoleon's chances of carrying on the Napoleonic line certainly seemed grim.[56]

[56] J. M. Thompson, *Louis Napoleon and the Second Empire* (Oxford: Basil Blackwell, 1954), 1-2.

Louis Phillipe

Louis Napoleon's mother was unloved and neglected by her husband, but she greatly admired the exiled Bonaparte. After Waterloo and his exile to St. Helena, "she was vowed to the cult of his memory; and in the mind of the boy of seven who was with her he was already beginning to shine as the patron saint of a Second Empire."[57]

By the age of 32, Louis Napoleon had attempted two coups, having sought to remove Louis Phillippe from the throne in 1836 and 1840. For his second attempt, Louis was given a life sentence, which he served in Ham in northern France, but the imprisonment did not end his attempts to ingratiate himself to the people of France, nor his ambition for power. In 1843, he wrote, "I have never believed, and I never shall believe that France is the property of a particular man or family. I have never claimed any rights but those of every French citizen. I shall never desire anything but to see the People as a whole choose with complete liberty the form of government that suits its taste."[58]

---

[57] Ibid., 10.
[58] Ibid., 67.

In truth, Louis Napoleon would take the throne as an inheritance if possible, but he would also clearly submit to an election if the political current of the day required it. During his imprisonment, he entertained the writings of Adam Smith, as well as visits from the leading utopian socialist, Louis Blanc.[59]

Louis Napoleon was a study in contrasts, but he was dedicated to power. He wrote of both his and his uncle's vision for France, "The Napoleonic idea is not one of war, but a social, industrial, commercial idea. If to some it appears always surrounded by the thunder of combats, that is because it was in fact too long veiled by the smoke of cannon and the dust of battles. Now the clouds are dispersed and we can see, beyond the glory of arms, a civil glory greater and more enduring…the Napoleonic idea has as many branches as there are phases of human genius. It revivifies agriculture, borrows useful inventions from foreign countries, levels mountains, spans rivers, promotes communications and compels nations to shake hands. It provides work for all men and all capacities; it enters the cottage, not holding forth barren declarations about the rights of man, but with means to slake the poor man's thirst, to satisfy his hunger and with a glorious story to awake his patriotism."

He had previously attempted a return to France to see his dying father, only to be refused because he would not sign a promise to give up his designs on the throne of France. Finally, his chance came in 1846, when he disguised himself as a workman and escaped the fortress at Ham while it was undergoing repairs.[60] He went straight to London, where he planned to wait out the French people's call for his return to France, and hopefully, to the throne.[61] Upon getting his freedom, however, he found himself frustrated by the wait and had little hope of his return at times. As he put it, "Nothing can be done at the moment…the nation is asleep, and will remain asleep for a long time yet. Whatever may be said, I have tried the only means of awakening it— the army; and I have failed hopelessly. I can't and won't try again: I must wait patiently for a better opportunity."[62]

By 1847, conditions in France had deteriorated, and though he was unaware at the time, Louis Phillipe's days were numbered. A simple dispute led to a student protest and the spread of outrage among Paris' workers. Making matters worse, the National Guard's refusal to act on the king's behalf meant that the French Army had to be summoned to Paris to put the uprising down. Rather than see the people of Paris slaughtered, Louis Philippe abdicated the throne and fled the city.[63]

Louis Napoleon immediately returned to France, only to find that the time was still not right for his ascent to power. The two failed attempts had made him more cautious, so he returned to

---

[59] Ibid., 67-8.
[60] Ibid., 71.
[61] Ibid., 73.
[62] Ibid., 83.
[63] Ibid., 85-86.

England, writing to the provisional government in Paris:

"Gentlemen,

"After 33 years of exile and persecution, I believed I had acquired the right to find once more a refuge on the soil of the fatherland. You think that my presence in Paris at this moment is embarrassing; I therefore withdraw for the time being. You must take this sacrifice as a sign of the purity of my intentions, and of my patriotism."[64]

In the face of a potentially violent revolution in the streets, a general election was held in 1848, and it resulted in Louis Napoleon getting 74% of the vote.[65] Though he was untested as a leader, the various coalitions - closet conservatives, republicans, and even socialists - hoped he would champion their policies. Though he disappointed the most radical of his supporters, Louis Napoleon's programs of reform, coupled with enough conservatism to maintain his power through coalitions and compromise, served to keep him in power. Wildly popular in his early reign, Louis Napoleon served as Emperor Napoleon III, reviving the grandiosity of imperial France for two decades.

The mid-1860s presented France with a new challenge in the form of Prussia, which was fast rising as a power. On May 27, 1866, the *New York Times* reported that "it is said that French officers who have recently examined the military resources of Prussia and the organization of her army report that there is not much chance of her success in a campaign against Austria and her German auxiliaries—in fact, that Prussia is no match for her rival."[66] In truth, France had greatly underestimated the power of its Prussian neighbor. Geoffrey Wawro, professor of military history at the University of North Texas, states that in response to the Austrian collapse in the face of the Prussian armies, "France gaped in astonishment. Almost overnight a rather small and manageable neighbor had become an industrial and military colossus."[67]

Napoleon's advisors were so sure of Prussia's weakness that they insisted he go to war against them immediately following their decisive victory at Koniggratz, where 44,000 Austrians were lost. This battle ended the Austrians' chances in what would only be a seven-week war, but Napoleon had expected the Austro-Prussian War to drag on, believing the two sides were far more evenly matched. This meant that at the time that conflict was winding down, the French armies were dispersed all over the world. There were "63,000 in Algeria, 28,000 in Mexico, 8,000 in Rome, and 2,000 in Indochina," which meant those forces were unavailable for a fight.[68] In fact, in July of 1866, the French would have been outnumbered by a much larger and more

[64] Ibid., 86.

[65] Matthew Truesdell, *Spectacular Politics: Louis-Napoleon Bonaparte and the Fete Imperiale, 1849-1870* (New York: Oxford University Press, 1997), 13.

[66] "Different Accounts of the Emperor's Speech at Auxerre: The Interpointed Passage- Military Strength of Prussia." *The New York Times.* May 27, 1866.

[67] Ibid., 17.

[68] Ibid., 18.

confident Prussian Army. For the time, open conflict between France and Prussia was averted.

In 1870, Napoleon III was in a tenuous position as French leader, and his popularity had fallen drastically. The French government, in its current state, could not afford to lose face amongst the world powers, but it also felt it could not afford to be surrounded by pro-Hapsburg rulers.[69] Bismarck's decision not to destroy the Austrians in peace negotiations at the end of the Austro-Prussian War meant there would be another rival to French power ruled by Germanic Hapsburgs.

Napoleon III believed the old powers of Europe were slowly dying, and that it was he who could build a united Europe by quietly encouraging nationalistic movements in Italy, Poland, and by the Czechs. These newly independent states would need France as an ally and protector, which would raise its profile as Europe's new ruler.[70] The Crimean War, in which a coalition of British and French badly defeated the Russians, helped to reduce Russian prestige with their surrender in 1856,[71] and Napoleon III hoped that a partial unification of northern Italy would allow him to rule the south. Instead, Italian nationalism scored a surprise victory under Camillo Cavour, King Victor Emmanuel, and southern nationalist Giuseppe Garibaldi. Italy was united as a modern nation-state in 1870.

To the west, Napoleon relied on his ability to maintain "that influence on neighbouring [sic] countries which was traditional to France."[72] When it came to Spain, the French relied on stable relations between the two countries for France's economic, political, and military health. Napoleon believed that if France lost Spain as an ally while facing a conflict with the Prussians, it would mean a loss of between 40,000 and 80,000 troops, as well as France's freedom of the seas. It could even bring about a French defeat in a war against Prussia.[73]

Queen Isabella II of Spain had been removed from the throne as the result of a revolution in 1868, and that put Napoleon III in the awkward position of attempting to influence and even control who succeeded her without appearing to be involved. Having successfully blocked two choices he found unacceptable, he eventually had to deal with "the Hohenzollern candidate," Leopold, Prince of Hohenzollern.[74] Despite assurances "there had not been, and never would be, a question of the Prince of Hohenzollern's accepting the Spanish crown" by Bismarck's undersecretary of state, by January of 1870, a suitable candidate for the Spanish throne had not been found. At this point, Bismarck decided to openly champion Leopold's cause.[75]

---

[69] Bertrand Taithe, *Citizenship and Wars: France in Turmoil, 1870-1* (London: Routledge, 2001), 8.
[70] Ibid.,9
[71] Ibid., 11.
[72] T. A. B. Corley, *Democratic Despot: A Life of Napoleon III* (London: Barrie and Rockliff, 1961), 321.
[73] Ibid., 322.
[74] Ibid.
[75] Ibid., 323.

Queen Isabella II

Leopold, Prince of Hohenzollern

According to conventional wisdom, Bismarck pursued Leopold's candidacy to provoke the French. As early as 1867, he entertained the idea that a French attack on Prussia, so long as it didn't involve any religious elements (since both France and southern Germany were strongly Catholic), could bring unity to all of Germany. As one writer noted, "The Hohenzollern candidature now presented an ideal pretext whereby he could inflict a crushing humiliation on France and, under the auspices of the King of Prussia, achieve the unification of Germany with the whole nation backing him in the struggle."[76] In his memoirs, Bismarck denied having a specific interest in Leopold as King of Spain, claiming instead that he believed the French would support the candidate whom he saw as friendly to the French "due to his personal and family connexions [sic] in Paris."[77] Bismarck wrote the following with respect to the question of the successor to the throne: "I regarded it as a Spanish and not as a German one, even though I was delighted at seeing the German name of Hohenzollern active in representing monarchy in Spain and did not fail to calculate all the possible consequences from the point of view of our interests—a duty which is incumbent on a foreign minister when anything of similar importance occurs in another state."[78]

[76] Ibid., 324.
[77] Otto Von Bismarck, *Bismarck, the Man and the Statesman Being the Reflections and Reminiscences of Otto, Prince Von Bismarck*, vol. II (New York: Harper & Brothers, 1898), 87.

Bismarck critics will smile at this "admission," which forms the basis of much of the criticism of Bismarck's *realpolitik*. Put simply, his decisions were ultimately made based on what worked for Bismarck's goals of German unity, whatever the topic and whatever the cause. According to Bismarck, the French were the ones who "proved...that the moment had arrived when France sought a quarrel against us and was ready to seize any pretext that seemed available."[79]

In the debate over Leopold's candidacy, French representative Gramont threatened Prussia, at least as Bismarck saw it. Gramont stated, "We do not believe that respect for the rights of a neighbouring [sic] people binds us to suffer a foreign Power to set one of its Princes on the throne of Charles V. This event will not come to pass, of that we are quite certain...Should it prove otherwise we shall know how to fulfil [sic] our duty without shrinking and without weakness."

In Bismarck's view, Gramont's response was "a hand on the sword hilt.[80] When it was announced that Leopold had officially withdrawn his name from consideration in response to French objections, Bismarck considered it the end of his career as a "responsible foreign minister."[81] For Bismarck, Prussian King Wilhelm I had humiliated both himself and Prussia in continuing to entertain French concerns through Gramont, and now war was only one way to save face.

---

[78] Ibid., 88.
[79] Ibid., 91.
[80] Ibid., 93.
[81] Ibid., 97.

Wilhelm I

Gramont

It was through Bismarck's alteration of an international communication that the Franco-Prussian War began in earnest. A telegram bearing the Prussian king's words was brought to Bismarck during a meeting with Prussian General Helmuth von Moltke and War Minister Albrecht von Roon. Its reading confirmed the worst regarding the outcome of the Prussian king's meetings with the French ambassador, and in his memoirs, Bismarck claimed that neither Moltke nor Roon could eat or drink after its reading: "M. Benedetti intercepted me on the Promenade in order to demand of me most insistently that I should authorize him to telegraph immediately to Paris that I shall obligate myself for all future time never again to give my approval to the candidacy of the Hohenzollerns should it be renewed. I refused to agree to this, the last time somewhat severely, informing him that one dare not and cannot assume such obligations *à tout jamais*. Naturally, I informed him that I had received no news as yet, and since he had been informed earlier than I by way of Paris and Madrid, he could easily understand why my government was once again out of the matter. Since then His Majesty has received a dispatch from the Prince [Charles Anthony]. As His Majesty has informed Count Benedetti that he was expecting news from the Prince, His Majesty himself, in view of the above-mentioned demand and in consonance with the advice of Count Eulenburg and myself, decided not to receive the French envoy again but to inform him through an adjutant that His Majesty had now received from the Prince confirmation of the news which Benedetti had already received from Paris, and that he had nothing further to say to the Ambassador. His Majesty leaves it to the judgment of Your Excellency whether or not to communicate at once the new demand by Benedetti and its rejection to our ambassadors and to the press."[82]

According to his memoirs, Bismarck now believed "war could be avoided only at the cost of the honour of Prussia and of the national confidence in it."[83] In response to "this conviction," Bismarck asserted, "I made use of the royal authorisation [sic] communicated to me through Abeken [an official dispatch writer], to publish the contents of the telegram; and in the presence of my two guests I reduced the telegram by striking out words, but without adding or altering."[84] Bismarck's wording, by his own admission, "made this announcement appear decisive, while Abeken's version would only have been regarded as a fragment of a negotiation still pending, and to be continued at Berlin:"[85]

Bismarck recorded his response openly and claimed that he had the right to amend the telegram and that it was the only answer for the Prussians, who would have otherwise had to "act the part of the vanquished without a battle."[86] According to Bismarck, von Moltke and von Roon went

---

[82] Louis L. Snyder, ed., Documents of German History. (New Brunswick, N.J.: Rutgers University Press, 1958), pp. 215-16.
[83] Otto Von Bismarck, 100.
[84] Ibid.
[85] Ibid., 101.
[86] Ibid.

from "revulsion" to "a more joyous mood" at the reading of Bismarck's version. Though Bismarck would face tension with Prussian military leadership during the war, he believed it was important to communicate not only his beliefs concerning the French but that the greatest Prussian military minds agreed with his thoughts about the necessity to fight the French.

Helmuth von Moltke

Albrecht von Roon

Bismarck's version of the Ems telegram arrived in Paris on July 14, and just five days later, the war began. Historians may lay responsibility for the war at Bismarck's feet, but many Germans believed they had been wronged. In the popular "Prayer in the German Defensive War," the innocence of the German cause was expressed:

> "O Sov'reign Lord of peace and war,
> To us a righteous war now sending,
> With heartfelt thanks thy throne before,
> See here thy children lowly bending.
>
> Not we the foe did e'er provoke,
> Nor rash our hands were now imbruing:
> With firm resolve we deal the stroke,
> What must be—that alone pursuing.
>
> We do not now unsheathe the brand,
> To vain presumptuous idly yielding:
> The foe has thrust it ion our hand—
> Give vict'try to the arms were yielding."[87]

The French, as with every other major power in 1866, had witnessed the devastation caused by the Prussian *Zundnadelgewehr,* or needle gun. Despite the gun's lack of accuracy, the ability of a soldier to reload far more rapidly and without exposure to return fire from having to stand or kneel to reload gave the Prussians an extreme advantage without which no country could fight future wars. Following the Austro-Prussian War, Napoleon III appointed a new minister of war and charged him with updating both weapons and strategy.[88] Geoffrey Wawro, a historian of the Franco-Prussian War and Austro-Prussian War, lists the advantages of a new French weapon, the Chassepot, over the very recently outdated Austrian needle gun, the Dreyse. In adopting the Chassepot as the standard military rifle, the French had:

- a longer and more effective range than Prussian weapons;
- a far lighter gun than the Dreyse, allowing a soldier to expend less energy when carrying the rifle;
- rounds that fired at 8 to 15 a minute as opposed to four to six for the Dreyse;
- bullets capable of massive destruction of the body, destroying bone and muscle; and

---

[87] Carl Weitbrecht, "Prayer in the German Defensive War 1870." *Translations from the German*, by Edward Stanhope Pearson. 1879.

[88] Geoffrey Wawro, 51-52.

- a smaller caliber of bullet, allowing the average French soldier to carry 105 bullets, compared to the Prussian who carried 70.

Perhaps most advantageous for the French, the Dreyse needle gun, despite its superiority in 1866, had a major flaw. Soldiers were loathe to fire the gun from either an upright or prone position due to the burns they often received from a leaky breech. With France's access to colonial rubber, the Chassepot was successfully sealed in its breech, ensuring the French soldiers would not be harmed by their own weapons.[89]

The Chassepot

Though the Chassepot was a better rifle than the Prussian soldiers had, the advantage in the practical use of artillery was with the Prussians. Despite having observed the steel, breech-loading Krupp gun at the Universal Exhibition, the French government was not in a financial position to purchase the guns for the army in 1867.[90] Instead, the French pursued the bronze Mitrailleuse, a weapon first developed in Belgium which saw large-scale use for the first time during the Franco-Prussian War. Often called the first machine gun, the Mitrailleuse was a weapon whose categorization is open to debate; too large and cumbersome to be considered a rifle, yet not large enough to be classified as a cannon, the Mitrailleuse required training and

[89] Ibid., 52-53.
[90] Bertrand Taithe., 7.

experience to be used effectively, as the French would discover to their detriment.[91]

The Mitrailleuse

The Mitrailleuse is a high-interest but sometimes overrated weapon in the eyes of military historians. With the bulk of the money being spent to outfit the French with Chassepot rifles, the Mitrailleuse was too expensive for France to purchase in bulk. The desire to keep the weapon's capacity secret also contributed, albeit unwittingly, to its ineffectiveness at the beginning of the war; since the weapon was financed with the French emperor's personal funds and was constructed across France to maintain secrecy, neither the guns nor their detailed instruction manuals were made available to French officers before the war. French General Achille Bazaine, the most experienced of the three main French generals during the war, claimed he had never seen a Mitrailleuse "until one was wheeled past him at the Battle of Sedan on 2 September 1870, nearly two months after war had been declared."[92]

[91] Patrick Marder, "The Mitrailleuse." Military History Online. January 29, 2006. Accessed 3 July 2018.
[92] Ibid.

Bazaine

Firing 25 rifle bullets in rapid succession, the Mitrailleuse had the potential to devastate an enemy, but the smaller Prussian military would simply not accept its ability to intimidate its soldiers. In a pamphlet published just prior to the war, the Prussian government mockingly assured the Prussian soldiers that there was no need to fear the new weapon: "The French have always tried, at the outbreak of a war to surprise the world and the enemy with something new. This time it is the Mitrailleuses, which are to bring us confusion and defeat, and to them victory. Never have the French had luck with the introduction of new weapons. The rifled cannon in Italy in 1859, initially feared and admired, fired over and past their targets, because their own people didn't know them, their artilleryman still couldn't have any confidence in them...As the French fired past the target in 1859, so they will in 1870 fire past the target, if they hope to surprise us with their weapon. We have tested the same one and established its true low value. If we had held it necessary, for the lifting of the moral element in our army, to have to do something, then perhaps we would also have introduced this weapon. But that was not the case. The most dangerous foe of every battery is and will always remain the skilled marksman, who knows how to approach under cover, takes a bead on artillerymen and draught horses and is followed by brave, densely formed supports who complete what he started. Here is necessary clear-sighted leadership and a skilled use of terrain. But it is easier to find the right way to a Mitrailleuse than to a battery firing canister—even though we truly already succeeded in this. Against the latter there [is] really no space that uncovered. The cone of dispersion of the projectiles spreads apart from one another. On the contrary, the Mitrailleuse fires from some twenty barrels of a common steel casing, the same number of bullets which fly towards the target in a dense sheath. Over 1200 paces away the projectiles lose so much power that only weak hits can be made."[93]

Though the Prussian propaganda regarding the Mitrailleuse greatly underestimated the weapon, they made some good points. With so few available for fighting (190 total at the war's outbreak), so little knowledge about its potential, and many other problems being faced by the French army, the Mitrailleuse would not have a significant impact on the Franco-Prussian War.

The French began mobilization on July 19, 1870, and the Prussian armies responded to the French offense indignantly. To them, Prussia's borders and honor were under attack. As a poem put it:

"A voice resounds like thunder-peal,
'Mid dashing waves and clang of steel:
The Rhine, the Rhine, the German Rhine!
Who guards to-day my stream divine?
Dear Fatherland, no danger thine;
Firm stand thy sons to watch the Rhine!

They stand, a hundred thousand strong,
Quick to avenge their country's wrong;
With filial love their bosoms swell,
They'll guard the sacred landmark well!
Dear Fatherland, no danger thine;
Firm stand thy sons to watch the Rhine!

The dead of an [sic] heroic race,
From heaven look down and meet this gaze;
He swears with dauntless heart, 'O Rhine,
Be German as this breast of mine!'
Dear Fatherland, no danger thine;
Firm stand thy sons to watch the Rhine!

While flows one drop of German blood,
Or sword remains to guard thy flood,

---

[93] "Zur Orientierung über die Französische Armeelbid", qtd. in The Mitrailleuse." Military History Online. January 29, 2006.

While rifle rests in patriot hand,
No foe shall tread thy sacred strand!
Dear Fatherland, no danger thine;
Firm stand thy sons to watch the Rhine!

And whether my heart in death does break,
French we will not let them you make,
Rich in water as is your flood,
So Germany is in heroes' blood!
Dear Fatherland, no danger thine;
Firm stand thy sons to watch the Rhine!

Our oath resounds, the river flows,
In golden light our banner glows;
Our hearts will guard thy stream divine:
The Rhine, the Rhine, the German Rhine!
Dear Fatherland, no danger thine;
Firm stand thy sons to watch the Rhine!

So lead us on, you are well-proved;
Trusting in God, reach for the sword,
Hail Wilhelm! Down with the brood!
And redeem dishonor with enemy blood!
Dear Fatherland, no danger thine;
Firm stand thy sons to watch the Rhine!"[94]

In his preparation for war, Napoleon III hoped for aid, if not some support from the Austrians, Italians, or Catholics of southern Germany, but he would be disappointed. The southern German states immediately joined with their northern Prussian comrades, and neither Austria nor Italy would risk openly supporting Napoleon III in the face of Prussia and Russia.[95]

Though Napoleon III traveled to the battlefield to lead the army, his health, age, and the conditions of his forces made the prospect ridiculous. Instead, he would choose a commander-in-chief, with the arrangements styled after the relationship between the Prussian king and General von Moltke, head of Prussian forces.[96] As Napoleon III's biographer, T. A. B. Corley, explained, "The one difficulty [for Napoleon III] was that he had nobody of the caliber of Moltke, a superb strategist who for years had been perfecting a plan to strike at the heart of

---

[94] Eva March Tappan, ed., The World's Story: A History of the World in Story, Song and Art, 14 vols., vol. 7, Germany, The Netherlands, and Switzerland. Boston: Houghton Mifflin, 1914, pp. 249-50.
[95] T. A. B. Corley, *Democratic Despot: A Life of Napoleon III* (London: Barrie and Rockliff, 1961), 336.
[96] Ibid., 337.

France should the occasion arise."[97]

Napoleon III had attempted military reforms throughout his time as French emperor, but long-standing tradition and various political coalitions alternatively supporting and attacking his leadership made change difficult. The French emperor and his coalition of reformers believed France was in need of a million men to defend France's borders, reliable allies in Russia and Britain, and a plan to quickly activate troops.[98] The French made significant progress in establishing a rail system with the potential to move its men, but as one historian noted, "the French high command seems to have believed that harnessing a nation's railroad network for mobilization consisted merely of ordering a unit to board a train at X and to off-load at Y. Nowhere was the difference between the 'theoretical' French and the 'technical' Germans more powerfully illustrated."[99]

Gary Cox, a professor of political science at Stanford University, rejected the notion that France made no preparations for war, or that they were unready. In fact, moving French soldiers from peacetime to war-footing was one of the major areas of focus in the reforms made during the late 1860s, accomplished by a 36 item "checklist" for mobilization. For Cox and other historians who agree, the blame for France's inability to successfully fight the Prussians should be laid at the feet of Napoleon III himself: "There was literally no one in the government or in the army to 'run the checklist' or to create and refine the checklist. The generalship of mobilization, like the generalship of campaigning, was the province of the commander alone."[100]

The French were undoubtedly outmatched as far as military leadership was concerned. General von Moltke, the strategic planner and military hero of 1866, had anticipated war with France ever since defeating the Austrians. Thanks to his concerns about France's ability to strike Prussia before the Prussians could fully prepare, General von Moltke spent his time advocating the construction of rail networks that would allow seven Prussian corps to quickly mobilize in the event of a war with France. Prussia would only be capable of withstanding a French attack by beating the French to the punch. By 1870, General von Moltke felt confident he had achieved his mobilization goals. The Prussians were able to meet an army of 70,000 Frenchmen (what General von Moltke estimated they could mobilize in 20 days) with three fully assembled corps.[101]

General von Moltke's strategy, developed in the four years between Prussia's war against Austria in 1866 and the outbreak of fighting with France in 1870, was an offensive one. Due to the far greater distances involved for the French to reach Berlin after crossing into German territory, compared to the 190 miles from Prussia's border to Paris, General von Moltke believed

---

[97] Ibid.
[98] Gary P. Cox, *The Halt in the Mud: French Strategic Planning from Waterloo to Sedan*, (Boulder, CO: Westview Press, 1994), 176-7.
[99] Ibid., 183.
[100] Ibid., 185.
[101] Ibid.,175.

mobilization was of utmost importance.[102]

Von Moltke's predictions, written several years before the war, envisioned a speedily mobilized Prussian force that would end its journey in Paris: "The operation against France will consist simply in our advancing, closed up as much as possible, a few marches into French territory until we meet the French Army and give battle. The general direction of this advance is Paris, because in that direction we are most certain to find our objective—the hostile army."[103]

Dealing with personal illness, division in his government, Parisians outraged by the Ems telegram, and his own grand visions, Napoleon III decided the best response to Prussia was to ignore his advisors' intricate and prepared war plans and assemble one great and intimidating army, to be led by the emperor himself. On July 28, 1870, he issued his Order of the Day for the troops assembled before him, which read, "Whatever may be the road we take beyond our frontiers, we shall come across the glorious tracks of our fathers. We shall prove worthy of them. All France follows you with its fervent prayers, and the eyes of the world are upon you. On our success hangs the fate of liberty and civilization."[104]

A painting of French reservists preparing for the war

[102] T.A.B. Corley, 337.
[103] Ibid.
[104] Michael Howard, *The Franco-Prussian War: The German Invasion of France 1870–1871.* (New York: Routledge, 1961),

August 1870

France's invasion of the German frontier proved a fatal mistake, so much so that the grand offensive was over almost before it began.

The war had begun with the Hohenzollern controversy, Bismarck's "deception," and an initial mobilization that left the French at a disadvantage. Though a cursory glance at the war is often followed by a discussion of the disaster at Sedan and Napoleon III's humiliating surrender, the war that set the tone for 20th century Europe's international relations has always deserved a closer look than it usually gets.

Napoleon was under pressure to move his army into Germany, and to take the offensive at the behest of his people. He responded by leading French forces across the Saar River to take the town of Saarbrucken, which he believed was not well-defended by the Prussians. Though he was correct that Saarbrucken's defenses were less prepared than the surrounding areas (in which von Moltke had concentrated the great Prussian force, as well as their new allies from the south), the Prussians fought to defend Saarbrucken and inflicted greater casualties than the number suffered. In the meantime, they prepared to defend the nearby strategic cities of Spicheren, Weissenburg, and Saarlouis.[105]

The Battle of Weissenburg a few days later has been described as "[t]he opening engagement of the campaign…between the advance-guard of the Third German Army, under the Crown Prince of Prussia, and a portion of French Marshal MacMahon's army…The Germans carried the French position, and captured the town of Weissenburg, at a cost of 91 officers and 1,460 men. The French lost 2,300 killed, wounded and prisoners."[106] The Prussian victory at Weissenburg allowed their forces to invade France, and with that, von Moltke's plans were coming to fruition.

On August 6, the Prussians decisively defeated the French at the Battle of Spicheren. "After an obstinate encounter, the French were driven from all their positions with heavy loss and compelled to retreat on Metz. The Germans lost 223 officers and 4,648 men…Five [French] companies maintained their position throughout the afternoon, in the face of a vastly superior force. This action is also known as the Battle of Forbach."[107] Unlike the French at Spicheren, the Prussians were reinforced, and the French were handed the first of two significant defeats on August 6, with the second being the Battle of Wörth.[108]

Napoleon III's plan to assemble an overwhelming French fighting force that would defeat the Prussians had been put in doubt during the first week of fighting, and the Battle of Wörth served to confirm this fact. Anxious to capitalize on the mood of war and to maintain his status as

---

[105] "Sarrbrucken." Franco-Prussian War.com
[106] "Franco-Prussian War." *Heritage History.* Accessed July 7, 2018.
[107] Ibid.
[108]108 "Spicheren." Franco-Prussian War.com

leader, Napoleon marched six divisions into Germany, taking the Saarland, but conditions deteriorated from there. An early supporter and later critic of the Franco-Prussian War, Fredrich Engels condemned Napoleon III for failing to carry out a "resolute advance" at the outset of the war in stark contrast with military experts who believed the French moved incautiously into Germany. He blamed the corruption of the French empire for the army's lack of readiness: "Why then, has no such forward movement taken place? For this good reason, that, if the French soldiers were ready, their commissariat was not…We have the evidence that the distribution of provisions for a campaign began on the first of August only; that the troops were short of field flasks, cooking tins, and other camping utensils; that the meat was putrid and the bread often musty. It will be said, we fear, that so far the army of the Second Empire has been beaten by the second Empire itself. Under a regime which has to yield bounties to its supporters by all the old regular established means of jobbery, it can not be expected that the system will stop at the intendance of the army. This war…was prepared long ago; the laying in of stores, especially equipments, was evidently one of the least conspicuous parts of the preparation; and yet at this very point such irregularities occur as to cause nearly a week's delay at the most critical period of the campaign."[109]

At Wörth, the Germans numbered 140,000, while the French forces mustered only 35,000. The other part of the force was located on the other side of the Vosges Mountains. Despite the French's initial resistance and the greater numbers of the Prussian force, combined with the effectiveness of German artillery in reducing French lines and firepower, the total German losses would amount to 10,000, while the withdrawing French force's losses were closer to 20,000. [110]

---

[109] "Frederick Engels on the Conduct of the Franco-Prussian War." Science & Society 5, no. 4 (1941): 362-72. http://www.jstor.org/stable/40399414.
[110] "Worth" Franco-Prussian War.com

A depiction of Prussian cavalry at the Battle of Wörth

Napoleon III ordered a retreat on August 7. He sent a telegram to his wife, Eugénie, back in Paris, informing her of the French defeat and instructing her to ready Paris to defend itself against the Germans. Eugénie replied with assurances, "I am sure that we will bring the Prussians the sword in the loins to the border. Courage therefore; with energy we will dominate the situation. I answer from Paris."[111]

---

[111] J. M. Thompson, Louis Napoleon and the Second Empire (Oxford: Basil Blackwell, 1954), 303.

Eugénie

The defeats at Spicheren and Wörth compelled the French generals to retreat, and as the French continued their mobilization efforts, the generals attempted to assimilate new troops, reorganize, and strategize as mid-August approached.[112] Napoleon III and his advisors debated whether he should return to Paris with the army or attempt to rescue the rest of the French forces under General Bazaine.

On his way to Verdun, General Bazaine was confronted by a small Prussian force on August 16. Believing that he was outnumbered, Bazaine retreated to the Fortress of Metz, despite outnumbering the Prussians 5-1.[113]

In the ensuing battle, both sides lost about 16,000, and it was at the Battle of Mars-la-Tour that the last of the great cavalry charges took place. Known as "the death ride of Von Bredow" after the German officer who led it, the charge was carried out by about 600 cavalrymen, acting under orders to protect the flank of the army at all costs. Riding under cover of smoke and fire, Adalbert von Bredow was said to have responded to the impossible task of charging the much larger French force's battery and infantry lines by acknowledging "it will cost what it will."

[112] Ibid., 304.
[113] "Battle of Mars la Tour." Franco-Prussian War.

The element of surprise worked in von Bredow's favor, and after running off or killing every man on the French battery lines, the cavalry reached the infantry lines. Without cover, they took many losses. Nevertheless, "outnumbered as they were, the German horsemen kept together and fought their way out of the melee. Then they rode back through a storm of fire—rifles, machine-guns, canon opened on them—and only a handful reached the German lines. 'They rode back—not the Six Hundred.' Two-thirds of the officers and men strewed the 300 yards of ground over which they had charged. Only 104 of the cuirassiers and 90 of the landers answered the roll-call."[114] Amazingly, von Bredow would survive the charge and earn a promotion.

A depiction of the famous charge

Not all battles in the Franco-Prussian War were easy Prussian victories. Gravelotte was the largest battle of the war, and probably the second most memorable, and it was brutally contested. Von Moltke's combined armies (about 188,000) faced Bazaine's French force of 112,000 men, and though it was ultimately a Prussian win, the effectiveness of French weaponry was evident, as the Prussians lost over 20,000 men to the Chassepot, the Mitrailleuse, and advance preparations on the part of the French. Relying on their artillery to support the attack, the Germans of the First Army pressed forward into the Mance Ravine.[115] It was there the French response took its heaviest toll: "All day long, from noon until nearly the going down of the sun, the roar of the cannon and the roll of musketry has been incessant. The deep ravine of the Mance

[114] A. Hilliard Atterridge. Modern Battles. (Boston: Small, Maynard, and Company, 1913), 160-1.
[115] "Gravelotte." Franco-Prussian War.com

between Gravelotte and St. Hubert was a horrible pandemonium wherein seethed masses of German soldiery, torn by the shell-fire of the French batteries, writhing under the string of the mitrailleuses [sic], bewildered between inevitable death in front and no less inevitable disgrace behind. Again and again frantic efforts were being made to force up out of the hell of the ravine and gain foothold on the edge of the plateau beyond; and ever the cruel sheet of lead beat them back and crushed them down."[116]

The arrival of the Second Army to cross the ravine at Mance meant the French needed to redouble their efforts. Archibald Forbes, a Scottish war correspondent, awaited the results of the battle with King Wilhelm I and Bismarck, writing, "High over the roll of the drums, the blare of the bugles, and the crash of the cannons rose the eager burst of cheering as the soldiers answered their sovereign's greeting, and then followed their chiefs down into the fell depths of the terrible chasm. The strain of the crisis was sickening as we waited for the issue in a sort of rapt spasm of somber [sic] silence. The old King sat with his back against a wall on a ladder, one end of which rested on a broken gun-carriage and the other on a dead horse. Bismarck, with an elaborate assumption of coolness which his restlessness belied, made a pretense to be reading letters. The roar of the close battle swelled and deepened, till the very ground trembled beneath us. The night fell like a pall, but the blaze of an adjacent conflagration lit up the anxious group here by the churchyard wall. From out the medley of broken troops littering the slope in front rose suddenly a great shout that grew in volume as it rolled nearer. The hoofs of a galloping horse rattled on the causeway. A moment later Moltke, his face for once quivering with excitement, sprang from the saddle, and running towards the King cried out: 'It is good for us; we have restored the position, and the victory is with Your Majesty!' The King sprang to his feet with a fervent 'God be thanked!' and then burst into tears. Bismarck with a great sigh of relief crushed his letters in the hollow of his hand; and a simultaneous Hurrah! welcomed the glad tidings."[117]

Unwilling to commit more men to a battle they now considered a defeat, the French retreated to Metz.

---

[116] Archibald Forbes, qtd. in J. M. Thompson, Louis Napoleon and the Second Empire (Oxford: Basil Blackwell, 1954), 305.
[117] Ibid., 305-6.

A depiction of Prussian soldiers at Gravelotte

Gravelotte all but made clear the French would suffer a humiliating defeat in the war, and in the wake of that battle, France's ambassador to London stated that Napoleon III's "opposition, restless as it was, would not stir up a revolution, for 'no party wishes to come into office with the risk of having to sign disastrous peace."[118] Instead, they hoped the emperor would agree to peace, placing the blame for the defeat upon his dishonored shoulders.

The Battle of Sedan

Though Bazaine's army still numbered 140,000 after Gravelotte, it was cut off from communication with Paris and already surrounded by a larger Prussian force. The Prussians made sure Metz would be inhospitable to the French, and as they headed to Paris after burying 9,000 men at Gravelotte, they were ready to put an end to the French both in Metz and the capital.[119]

Faced with the terrible consequences of Gravelotte, Napoleon III gave up command of his army to Bazaine. In a document signed at Chalons, Napoleon III gave command of Paris to General Louis-Jules Trochu, making him both governor and commander-in-chief of the forces assigned to defend the capital.[120]

Napoleon III left Metz and Bazaine in time to avoid being trapped, but General Patrice de MacMahon received orders from Paris to rescue Bazaine's army. Though historians agree that

---

[118] A. Hilliard Atteridge, 338.
[119] Geoffrey Wawro, 186-7.
[120] Archibald Wilberforce, The Great Battles of All Nations: From Marathon to Santiago 490 B.C to A.D. 1898. Vol. 2. (New York: Peter Fenelon Collier, 1898), 854.

MacMahon's movement toward Metz - and thus, Sedan - ultimate defeat for the French, Bazaine's promise that he was about to break his army out of Metz to join forces with MacMahon for a great push against the Prussians convinced many French they could still win. That included the doomed MacMahon, who steered the only French army that still had freedom of movement toward Metz.[121]

In his account of the Battle of Sedan, fought at the end of August, Captain Fitz-George wrote that though the ultimate surrender of Napoleon III and the siege of Paris came after the Battle of Sedan, the decisive battle should still be considered "the final disaster that befell the armies of the third Napoleon III."[122]

Military historian James Whitman credits four Prussians for the military preparedness that culminated with the major Prussian victory at Sedan. Albrecht von Roon, who had enforced conscription into the Prussian armies, ensured that every able-bodied Prussian was prepared to go to war for the king. Then there was the king himself, who inspired feelings of loyalty. Of course, it was General von Moltke who pulled off an encirclement strategy that led to the kind of complete success rarely achieved in military history,[123] and behind all of it was Bismarck, the 19th century's master statesman.[124]

With Bazaine licking his wounds after Gravelotte and the disintegrating standards of conduct amongst the French armies, there seemed two choices before the Battle of Sedan. The remainder of the French force could head back to defend Paris, or there could be an attempt to rescue Bazaine's army at Metz and press forward against the Prussians.[125] For Captain Fitz-George, the blame of choosing "folly" and pursuing the latter was due to political leaders, not the military generals; he believed the French empress and her Parisian advisors were more concerned about saving Napoleon III's life and the crown for their son than victory for the French armies.

For those who welcomed Napoleon III's demise, the fight at Sedan "evoke[d] pictures of a trapped army, of veterans fighting desperately to cut a way out by hand-to-hand fighting and furious cavalry charges, while untrained recruits stand immobile and suffering under a rain of shells; of incompetent generals wrangling in front of a sick Emperor; …emotions of desertion, of desperation, and of anger at the men governing the Second Empire who had brought France to such a pass."[126]

---

[121] Geoffrey Wawro, 186.

[122] Captain Fitz-George, A *Plan of the Battle of Sedan, Accompanied by a Short Memoir*. (London: Edward Stanford, 1871), 1.

[123] James Q. Whitman, *The Verdict of Battle: The Law of Victory and the Making of Modern War*. (Boston: Harvard University Press, 2012), 215.

[124] Richard Walden Hale, Jr., *Democratic France: The Third Republic from Sedan to Vichy*. (New York: Coward-McCann, 1941), 10.

[125] Captain Fitz-George., 22.

[126] Richard Walden Hale, Jr., *Democratic France: The Third Republic from Sedan to Vichy* (New York: Coward-McCann, 1941), 3.

The Prussians intercepted MacMahon's army on the way to Metz, and by August 23, Prussia's Prince Frederick Charles had Bazaine's army surrounded at Metz.[127] In his work on the war, historian Geoffrey Wawro put much of the blame on Bazaine, citing his lack of desire for bold decision-making, "consoling himself with familiar routines," and laziness in the face of the approaching Prussians.[128] Other historians place the blame for MacMahon's defeat at either Napoleon III's feet or those of the empress, who had directed MacMahon to save Bazaine's army at all costs. For Fitz-George, MacMahon lost the opportunity to move quickly against the Crown Prince and give Bazaine a chance to escape from Metz because "his heart was not in the march, and his troops were influenced by his slowness."[129]

Regardless of these differences of opinion, it is clear the French suffered from a lack of inspiration and hope, As Fitz-George put it, "the smart, dashing men whom we have seen when we travelled [sic] through France were reduced to a condition of semi-shabbiness and blank despondency which was something new to see. They were wont to be the gayest fellows in the world, and here were rolled up, tumbled over, and generally 'done for,' by men whom they had been rash enough to despise."[130]

By September 1, "the remnants of MacMahon's army, and the Emperor with them, were penned like sheep into the little town of Sedan, within the narrow circle of hills which afforded its only rampart."[131] On September 2, MacMahon was injured by a shell splinter in his thigh[132] early in the morning and command was handed over to his second, General Ducrot.[133] In the final battle of the war itself, German artillery continually bombarded the French armies until there was no hope left.[134] The Prussians attacked the town in the late afternoon, and after inflicting French losses of 20,000,[135] they entered Sedan to discover Napoleon III himself.[136]

Von Moltke had entrapped the French with multiple armies converging on the French forces between Sedan and the Belgian border. The Prussian armies were unable to push the French into Sedan, nor were they able to completely surround them with a Prussian force at the French's rear. By noon on September 1, the French were faced with a desperate situation. While the Prussian officers lunched with American observer Philip Sheridan, a note asking for surrender was sent to General MacMahon. He replied, asking for terms.

---

[127] Captain Fitz-George, 27.

[128] Geoffrey Wawro, 196.

[129] Captain Fitz-George, 28.

[130] Ibid., 77.

[131] J. M. Thompson, *Louis Napoleon and the Second Empire* (Oxford: Basil Blackwell, 1954), 307.

[132] Richard Walden Hale, Jr., Democratic France: The Third Republic from Sedan to Vichy (New York: Coward-McCann, 1941), 7.

[133] Ibid.

[134] D. W. Brogan, France under the Republic: The Development of Modern France (1870-1939) (New York: Harper & Brothers Publishers, 1940), 30.

[135] Ibid.

[136] J.M. Thompson, 308.

The French cavalry, both desperate and brave, attempted multiple futile breakouts to the south and north of their position, but this only resulted in more death as they "tried again and again to smash into the solid lines of infantry in the face of repeating rifles spitting a hail of bullets, crashing to the ground as they galloped downhill in the graveyard of lily."[137]

4. - Bataille de Sedan. - Un épisode du combat de La Moncelle, 1er Septembre 1870

A picture of the battle

General Wimpffen arrived with a letter from French Empress Eugénie, authorizing him to take control of the armies. He ordered the outraged Ducrot to stand down and reversed battle directions. Instead of a break-out order with the armies moving west, they were now to fight a fresh defense of Bazailles. Confused, the armies, demoralized and all but defeated, looked less attractive to Ducrot and Wimpffen, who, "when they realized the completeness of the defeat…reversed their positions and tried to foist on each other the ignominy of signing terms of surrender."[138]

Despite the many French defeats in August, Sedan stands out for the "sheer size of the French forces surrendered," at over 80,000 men.[139] For the Germans, what would become known as "Sedan Day" served as the equivalent of America's Fourth of July, and the founding day of Germany itself.[140]

The French defeat would also serve to create the conditions for a new and united Germany to seize Alsace-Lorraine, which most Germans thought was rightfully theirs. To convince the British of Germany's reasonable decision to take Alsace-Lorraine, Thomas Carlyle wrote,

---

[137] Richard Walden Hale, 5.
[138] Ibid., 8.
[139] James Q. Whitman, *The Verdict of Battle: The Law of Victory and the Making of Modern War.* (Boston: Harvard University Press, 2012), 215, 7.
[140] Ibid., 208.

"Germany, I do clearly believe, would be a foolish nation not to think of raising up some secure boundary-fence between herself and such a neighbor now that she has the chance." Whether they saw the taking of Alsace-Lorraine as restoring previous territory (from 1582), a safety measure against future French aggression, or a "just reward for national victory,"[141] Alsace-Lorraine would be German once more.[142]

In the late stages of the fighting at Sedan, Napoleon III wrote to the Prussian king, "My brother, having been unable to die in the midst of my troops, it remains for me to put my sword in the hands of your Majesty. I am from your Majesty the good brother Napoleon III."[143] Not only did von Moltke demand the surrender of Napoleon III, but that of the entire French army. Though Napoleon III met with both Bismarck and King Wilhelm I in an attempt to get less draconian terms, the Prussians pressed their advantage, threatening to bombard Sedan again the next morning unless the French laid down their arms.[144]

In response, Napoleon III asserted that he had no power to speak for France: "I have no power. I am a prisoner." Instead, the Prussians would have to speak with the new government: "In Paris, the Empress and the Ministers have alone power to treat. I am powerless. I can give no orders, and make no conditions."

On the evening of his surrender, Napoleon III wrote of Sedan and his surrender to his wife, "My dear Eugénie, I cannot tell you what I have suffered and am suffering. We made a march contrary to all the rules and to common sense: it was bound to lead to a catastrophe, and that is complete. I would rather have died than have witnessed such a disastrous capitulation; and yet, things being as they are, it was the only way of avoiding the slaughter of 60,000 men. Then again, if only all my torments were concentrated here! I think of you, of our son, of our unfortunate country. May God protect you! What is going to happen at Paris? I have just seen the King. There were tears in his eyes when he spoke of the sorrow I must be feeling. He has put at my disposal one of his *châteaux* near Hesse-Cassel. But what does it matter where I go? I am in despair. *Adieu*; I embrace you tenderly."[145]

---

[141] Geoffrey Wawro, 230.
[142] Ibid.
[143] J.M. Thompson, 308.
[144] Ibid., 308-9.
[145] Ibid., 310.

A depiction of Napoleon III meeting with Bismarck

The Final Resistance

Fearful for her life and safety now that her husband was a prisoner of war, Eugénie sought protection with an American dentist practicing in Paris.[146] By September 4, Eugénie's chief protector, General Trochu, had abandoned his defense of the regent to become president of the new Third Republic. Her few loyal advisors convinced her to immediately depart from the palace.

Her escape (aided by the Ambassador of Italy, Metternich of Austria, a few loyal officials, and her court) was narrow, while the mob shouted, "Down with the Spaniard! To the guillotine!" Once outside the palace and in the streets, Eugénie was placed in a taxi with the loyal Madame Lebreton, and after being turned away at the residences of former friends, Eugénie chose the home of Dr. Evans, the American dentist she hoped would assist her.[147]

Evans had met Napoleon III as a 24-year-old dental intern, but through his dentistry and social artistry, he rose to become a member of Napoleon III's court, having even attended Eugénie and Napoleon III's wedding in 1853. Evans was highly favored by the court and was used to communicate with noble and royal families of neighboring nations when Napoleon III desired a backchannel. Through the gifts bestowed on him and the patronage of Europe's highest circle, Evans invested in real estate, and he was a millionaire in 1870 when the empress came to his

[146] Gerald Carson, "The Dentist and the Empress." American Heritage. Vol. 31, Issue 4. June/July 1980.
[147] Ibid.

home in disguise.[148]

Eugénie made her case to the surprised doctor, telling him, "Monsieur, I have no friends left but you. I come as a fugitive to beg your help. I am no longer fortunate. The evil days have come, and I am left alone."[149]

Dr. Evans and his wife spirited Eugénie out of France to England, where she was reunited with her 14-year-old son, whom she had always hoped would be heir to the throne of France.

The Battle of Sedan can be found in many historians' lists of the most decisive battles in history, but the French themselves still held out hope, even as Bismarck and King Wilhelm I believed they could negotiate an end to the war with Napoleon III. However, Napoleon III's position of weakness meant he could not bring the war to an end in 1870. Napoleon III's biographer believed the former emperor may have wanted to deal with the Prussians (his wife even more so to earn conditions favorable to her son's eventual ascension), but Napoleon III refused to compromise on "three principles." He would not order Bazaine (who remained at Metz with 150,000 men) to surrender, he would not put his own future ahead of the French people, and he would sign nothing dishonoring France.[150]

As Napoleon III dealt with the Prussians, the French declared a Third Republic that would last until World War II. Napoleon III's creation, the Legislative Body, went into a midnight session where the call to end his reign would be heeded. Though there had been no official announcements about the defeat of the French armies, rumors swirled through Paris, and crowds formed outside the Palace Bourbon, where the legislative body was meeting, to demand an end to Napoleon III's reign.

Without the soldiers' support, there was little the Assembly could do to calm the crowds gathering outside in the Place de la Concorde. With the soldiers' help, the mob pushed into the meeting place of the National Assembly despite the Republicans' attempt to abate the crisis and gain time to redistribute power, while "[i]nside the chamber [Republican leader] Leon Gambetta...tried to shoo away the invaders."[151] He begged, "What I ask of you is that you should feel, as I do the extreme gravity of the situation, and that you should not disturb us by your cries, or even by your applause...There are two things to be done: the first, that the Representatives should come back and take their places on these seats, and the second, that the meeting should be held in the usual way, so that, discussion being entirely free, the decision arrived at should be of a nature to entirely satisfy the conscience of France...Remember that the stranger is upon our soil. It is in the name of our country, and in the name of political liberty— two things that I, for one, shall never separate—it is in the name of these great interests, and as a

[148] Ibid.
[149] Ibid.
[150] T. A. B. Corley, 347.
[151] Geoffrey Wawro, 232.

representative of the French nation, which is able to make itself respected at home as well as abroad, that I adjure you to be quiet while your representatives come back to their seats."[152]

Gambetta

The mob would have none of it. "They gruffly pushed passed him…The demonstrators streamed through the half-empty chamber. Some gaped at the rich furnishings, others seated themselves at the desks, doodling on the official stationery, or simply rested their rifles on the floor and chanted for the republic."[153]

This new provisional government was doomed from the beginning. Dealing with a defeated French army, economic crisis, a lack of trust from the people, and the demands of the radical Parisian left, they concentrated their efforts on personal survival in the days to follow.

The new republic, without support and without direction, was left to negotiate the terms of peace. To start, the idea of a German Alsace-Lorraine was not acceptable to anyone in France; even the weakened Mayor of Paris Jules Favre would "cede neither a clod of our earth, nor a stone of our fortresses" to the Germans.[154]

---

[152] Frank T. Marzials, *Life of Leon Gambetta*. (London: W.H. Allen and company, 1890), 66.
[153] Geoffrey Wawro, 232.
[154] Ibid., 235.

They would need to defeat Paris, but an offensive against the city would need an army three times the size of the French defenders' force to take the capital city. In early September, von Moltke's forces numbered 240,000 men.[155] The Germans also faced the complication of supplying troops in France's interior and maintaining morale, having been warned by King Wilhelm I, "There is much bloody work ahead of us."[156]

Desperate to starve out the Germans before the resistance crumbled, the French took extreme measures. "To cause the German besiegers maximum difficulty, Trochu ordered the destruction of all roads, canals, bridges, and railways out to a distance of fifty miles. Closer in, he devastated the land by burning farms, razing villages, and slaughtering livestock to deny Germans food and shelter. The siege of Paris was a race against time and resources, but it was also a world opinion, as some nations were sympathetic to the French's plight, and some believed a united German empire would be a danger for future peace."[157]

Still staving off surrender at Metz, the French armies had consumed their supplies and were eating their own horses to survive. Vainly awaiting Bazaine's outbreak and rescue of Paris, the Parisians, too, began to starve. On October 27, 1870, Bazaine agreed to surrender his men to the Germans, reinforcing his reputation as a failed leader through his inaction. Bazaine allowed his officers to remain at Metz (as the Germans had offered) after surrendering to the enemy and arranging the safety of both himself and his wife.[158]

Bazaine's surrender of nearly 140,000 French troops left Paris to its own defenses. In many ways, Paris hoped for a direct assault by German forces on the city, which they believed would rally the city to its defense, negate international support for the German armies, and give the French soldiers - ironically just now ready for battle - who had been called up in July a fresh chance at a military victory.

Instead, the Germans waited for the siege to do its ugly work.[159] Not only did the siege cut Paris off from most of its supplies, it cut off the capital from information, as well. This meant the new government often operated blind, leaving the people dependent on rumors. Though Favre, Trochu, and others in the provisional government were afraid of mobs, and rightfully so, they encouraged them to attack German soldiers and units whenever possible,[160] hoping that early morning surprise raids at the borders would wear down German morale.[161]

The lack of outside information, food, and direction from the government left the people to

---

[155] Ibid., 237.
[156] Ibid., 234.
[157] Ibid., 234.
[158] Ibid., 251.
[159] Mike Duncan, "The Siege of Paris". Revolutions. Podcast audio, 27 May, 2018.
    <http://www.revolutionspodcast.com/2018/05/84-the-siege-of-paris.html>
[160] Ibid.
[161] Geoffrey Wawro, 237.

their own devices, and they formed committees that would see to the defenses of their own quarter of the city, as well as ration and distribute food, which had quickly become a key issue.[162] The committees ranged in political persuasion from those with loyalty to the republican government, to reformers, socialists, and outright Communists. The leftist communities would form the Paris Commune by March.

Desperate to both send and receive news of the French's fate at Metz, the condition of the French armies, and a list of much-needed supplies, the government used hot air balloons. 66 flights, some carrying homing pigeons able to fly undetected with the information, were sent successfully from Paris. On October 7, 1870, Leon Gambetta, then serving as the embattled Minister of the Interior,[163] left the city in a hot air balloon.[164] His goals were to whip up defenders who would open a new front to the war in the Loire Valley, providing increased morale and pulling Germans forces away from the siege. He boarded *L'Armands Barbes* "to a great shout of '*Vive la Republique! Vive Gambetta*'…When [the balloon] got beyond the line of the French forts…they became a mark for the rifles and cannon of the enemy, fortunately without result. Then the balloon…manifested a tendency to descend in too close proximity to the Germans, and was shot at again, and almost hit; and then, soon afterwards, another ineffectual volley was discharged at it."[165] Though Gambetta made it safely to Amiens, where he worked to continue the resistance, the news from Metz and the collapse of the government-in-exile at Tours meant his mission was futile.

While the provisional government under Jules Favre continued to hold out, deteriorating conditions would bring the public support of this government to an end. The excitement of a republic faded in the realities of a Parisian winter without food or supplies, and the city turned to eating anything available. Zoo animals were consumed, cats and rats were parts of the Parisians' regular diet, and even the Communists quietly agreed to a free market in scavenged meat.[166] Only the privileged could afford to buy even that much. The poor survived on allotments of hardened bread, which brought insurrections and a violent crackdown by the provisional government at the end of November, leading to the deaths of 9,000 revolutionaries.[167]

Finally, in January 1871, Bismarck convinced the king that the siege needed acceleration if the Germans were to be done with the war. With that, they began to shell Paris on January 6. On January 18, 1871, France was handed their greatest humiliation to date when German King Wilhelm I was declared emperor of a new, united Germany in Versailles' Hall of Mirrors.

Though the provisional government held onto power for a few more weeks, Paris boiled with

---

[162] Mike Duncan.

[163] Patrick H. Hutton, Amanda S. Bourque, and Amy J. Staples, eds., *Historical Dictionary of the Third French Republic, 1870-1940*, vol. 1 (Westport, CT: Greenwood Press, 1986), 410.

[164] Mike Duncan.

[165] Frank T. Marzials, 83.

[166] Mike Duncan.

[167] Ibid.

humiliation, anger, and resentment. The government determined that a dissolution of the National Guard, still heavily armed from the siege, was necessary. In mid-March, a firefight broke out during an attempt to seize cannons, leading to the death of two French generals at the hands of workers in Montmartre.

The fallout of this incident led to the establishment of the Paris Commune, which would rule Paris until May 28. The Commune would leave a lasting impression on historians and political figures, many of whom saw it as representative of their cause. Karl Marx viewed it as the rise of Communism, while others saw anarchism.[168] Naturally, commentary on the short-lived experiment is riddled with bias, from Karl Marx's *On the Paris Commune*, which paints the body as the precursor of utopian socialist promises, to those who believed the real unity of the Commune was found in its hatred of organized religion.[169]

The Commune remains controversial today, and historians continue to debate its origin and significance. Its members accused the provisional government of weakness, as well as a plot to restore the monarchy, claiming they were patriotic defenders of the French Republic against its corrupt leadership. When the government moved its operations out of Paris and began to restrict the freedom of the press, it gave the revolutionary movement energy. Meanwhile, its enemies saw it as a gang of rabble-rousers, exploiting the post-war situation to gain power for their radical leftist agenda. The Communards, as they were called, were divided into three groups: those interested primarily in the Paris Commune; those who believed a series of communes throughout France should rule; and extremists who believed violence was necessary to cleanse France.[170] Leaders of the Commune "proclaimed that since March 18, Paris "has no other government than that of the people, and this is the best one. Paris is free. Centralized authority no longer exists.""[171]

Within Paris, the Commune ruled in the absence of challenges. Wealthier workers and business people began to clear out of Paris, with over 200,000 leaving the city in fear of the violence of the mobs and their leaders. The Commune's actions ranged from the political, such as enacting new laws against religious displays and the clergy, to the economic, including abolishing rents and limiting the number of hours the city's bakers would work in the daylight hours. It also made military preparations to deal with Aldophe Thiers, the new president of the Republic, and the gathering Army of Versailles.

When the army finally arrived and entered an undefended section of Paris on May 21, the Communards resisted and "the bloody week" began. The number of dead is still a matter of

---

[168] Mitchell Abidor, *Voices of the Paris Commune*. (Oakland, CA: PM Press, 2015), i-iv.

[169] Adam Gopnik, "The Fires of Paris." The New Yorker. December 22 and 29th, 2014.

[170] The Editors of Encyclopaedia Britannica. "The Paris Commune." Chicago: *Encyclopaedia Britannica*, March 11, 2018. Accessed August 11, 2018.

[171] John Merriman, *Massacre: The Life and Death of the Paris Commune 1871*. (New Haven: Yale University Press, 2014), 49.

debate. While the army and Versailles government have been criticized for the unnecessary show of force, many died in terrible fires set by revolutionaries, many of them women. Casualty rates range in estimates from 6,000-50,000. The Tuileries Palace was burned to the ground, monuments to Napoleon III were toppled, and the Empress' former quarters were opened to tourists and deserters. On the other side, as the *New York Times* made clear on May 28, 1871, the Versailles government's supporters meant to leave no doubt that the revolution had been crushed: "Executions of insurgents are constant. The destruction of property is terrible. One-fourth of Paris is estimated to have been destroyed…A dispatch from St. Denis, Friday night, says there are still terrible conflagrations in Paris, the flames of which rise to a great height and illuminate the country for miles around. All human aid seems valueless."[172]

Victor Hugo's *Sur une Barricade* tells the story of the executions at the now famous "Communard Wall," where 147 revolutionaries made a last stand against the army. After being crushed, they were executed and put into a shallow grave. In Hugo's romantic account, a young boy is saved from execution when the shamed soldiers recognize his extraordinary bravery, despite their lack of faith in his cause:

"Soiled with guilty blood and pure blood washed,
A child of twelve is taken with men.
—Are you one of those, you?—The child says: We are.
'It's good,' said the officer, 'we'll shoot you.'
Wait your turn.—The child sees flashes of lightning,
And all his companions fall under the wall.
He said to the officer: Do you allow me to go
Bring this watch back to my mother at home?
—Do you want to run away?—I will be back.—These thugs
Are afraid! Where do you sleep?—There, near the fountain.
And I will come back, Captain.
—Go away, funny!—The child is leaving.—Rude trap!
And the soldiers were laughing with their officer,
And the dying mingled their laughter with this laugh;
But the laugh stopped, because suddenly the pale child,
Suddenly reappeared, proud as Viala,
He leaned against the wall and said: Here I am."[173]

The extinguishing of the Commune and the Germans' desire to be done with it all brought the end of the war. France was destroyed in both body and spirit; for Thomas Carlyle, a long observer of French history, the crushing of the Commune and the final defeat of the French in 1871 was just one more in a long line of disappointments from which the French would again

[172] David W. Dunlap. "1871: The Paris Agony." Looking Back in *The New York Times*. November 19, 2015.
[173] Victor Hugo, *Collected Works of Victor Hugo*. (Delphi Press, 2013).

suffer. "Poor France, one could observe all the while had, in spite of its boastings and the rumours [sic] of the Editors, no success in any enterprise whatever; and every "Victory", each in its turn, turned out within two days to have been a defeat cloaked by lies and fallacious hope. Poor France, what a bitter cup she is getting to drink! But it is of her own brewing; let us hope only that all these frightful sufferings may prove instructive to her and spare her more of the like!"[174]

Napoleon III would die within two years of the war's end, having never returned to France. On his deathbed, questions of his personal legacy remained, and he asked, "Isn't it true that we weren't cowards at Sedan?"[175] Not surprisingly, in retrospect, Napoleon III bemoaned the war's outcome: "I hoped Metz would have been left to us and that the war indemnity would not have exceeded three milliards. Such a peace can only be a truce and a fine prelude to troubles in Europe."

Napoleon III also looked forward, and he made a prescient commentary that predicted the conflict to come: "In spite of herself, Prussia in twenty or thirty years' time will be forced to become aggressive. Then, Europe will crush her."[176]

Online Resources

Other books about German history by Charles River Editors

Other books about French history by Charles River Editors

Other books about the Franco-Prussian War on Amazon

Further Reading

Abidor, Mitchell. *Voices of the Paris Commune*. Oakland, CA: PM Press, 2015.

Atterridge, A. Hilliard. *Modern Battles*. Boston: Small, Maynard, and Company, 1913.

"Battle of Mars la Tour." Franco-Prussian War.

Bismarck, Otto Von. *Bismarck, the Man and the Statesman Being the Reflections and Reminiscences of Otto, Prince Von Bismarck, Vol. II*. New York: Harper & Brothers, 1898.

Brogan, D. W. *France under the Republic: The Development of Modern France 1870-1939*. New York: Harper & Brothers Publishers, 1940.

---

[174] Qtd in Catherine Heyrendt, "A Rain of Balderdash": Thomas Carlyle and Victorian Attitudes toward the Franco-Prussian War," Carlyle Studies Annual 22, no. 2006 (2006).

[175] Louis Girard, *Napoléon III*, (Paris: Fayard, 1986), 500.

[176] T.A.B. Corley, 349.

Carlyle, Thomas. *The Works of Thomas Carlyle: Volume 30, Critical and Miscellaneous Essays V*, Volume 6. London: Cambridge University Press, 2010.

Carson, Gerald. "The Dentist and the Empress." *American Heritage*. Vol. 31, Issue 4. June/July 1980.

Corley, T. A. B. *Democratic Despot: A Life of Napoleon III*. London: Barrie and Rockliff, 1961.

Cox, Gary P. *The Halt in the Mud: French Strategic Planning from Waterloo to Sedan*. Boulder, CO: Westview Press, 1994.

---. "Different Accounts of the Emperor's Speech at Auxerre: The Interpointed Passage-Military Strength of Prussia." The New York Times. May 27, 1866.

Duncan, Mike. "The Siege of Paris". *Revolutions.* Podcast audio, 27 May, 2018. <http://www.revolutionspodcast.com/2018/05/84-the-siege-of-paris.html>

Dunlap. David W. "1871: The Paris Agony." Looking Back in *The New York Times*. November 19, 2015.

Fitz-George, Captain, *A Plan of the Battle of Sedan, Accompanied by a Short Memoir*. London: Edward Stanford, 1871.

"Franco-Prussian War." Heritage History. Accessed July 7, 2018.

"Frederick Engels on the Conduct of the Franco-Prussian War." *Science & Society* 5, no. 4 (1941): 362-72. http://www.jstor.org/stable/40399414.

Girard, Louis. *Napoléon III*, Paris: Fayard, 1986.

Gopnik, Adam. "The Fires of Paris." *The New Yorker.* December 22 and 29th, 2014.

"Gravelotte." Franco-Prussian War.com

Hale, Jr., Richard Walden. *Democratic France: The Third Republic from Sedan to Vichy.* New York: Coward-McCann, 1941.

Heyrendt, Catherine. "A Rain of Balderdash: Thomas Carlyle and Victorian Attitudes toward the Franco-Prussian War", Carlyle *Studies Annual* 22, no. 2006 (2006).

Howard, Michael. *The Franco-Prussian War: The German Invasion of France 1870–1871*. New York: Routledge, 1961.

Hugo, Victor. *Collected Works of Victor Hugo*. Delphi Press, 2013.

Hutton, Patrick H., Bourque, Amanda S. and Amy J. Staples, eds., *Historical Dictionary of the Third French Republic, 1870-1940*, vol. 1, Westport, CT: Greenwood Press, 1986.

Marder, Patrick. "The Mitrailleuse." Military History Online. January 29, 2006. Accessed 3 July 2018.

Marzials, Frank T. *Life of Leon Gambetta*. London: W.H. Allen and Company, 1890

Merriman, John. *Massacre: The Life and Death of the Paris Commune 1871*. New Haven: Yale University Press, 2014.

---. "Sarrbrucken." Franco-Prussian War.com

Snyder, Louis L. ed., *Documents of German History.* New Brunswick, N.J.: Rutgers University Press, 1958.

"Spicheren." Franco-Prussian War.com

Taithe, Bertrand. *Citizenship and Wars: France in Turmoil, 1870-1871* London: Routledge, 2001.

Tappan, Eva March ed., *The World's Story: A History of the World in Story, Song and Art*, 14 vols., vol. 7, Germany, The Netherlands, and Switzerland. Boston: Houghton Mifflin, 1914.

The Editors of Encyclopaedia Britannica. "The Paris Commune." Chicago: Encyclopaedia Britannica, March 11, 2018. Accessed August 11, 2018.

Thompson, J. M. *Louis Napoleon and the Second Empire* Oxford: Basil Blackwell, 1954.

Truesdell, Matthew. *Spectacular Politics: Louis-Napoleon Bonaparte and the Fete Imperiale, 1849-1870* New York: Oxford University Press, 1997.

Tucker, Spencer C. *500 Great Military Leaders.* Santa Barbara, California: ABC-CLIO LLC, 2015.

Wawro, Geoffrey. *The Franco-Prussian War: The German Conquest of France in 1870-1871.* Cambridge: Cambridge University Press, 2003.

"Weissenbourg." Franco-Prussian War.com

Weitbrecht, Carl. "Prayer in the German Defensive War 1870." Translations from the German, by Edward Stanhope Pearson, 1879.

Whitman, James Q. *The Verdict of Battle: The Law of Victory and the Making of Modern War.* Boston: Harvard University Press, 2012.

Wilberforce, Archibald. *The Great Battles of All Nations: From Marathon to Santiago* 490 B.C to A.D. 1898. Vol. 2. New York: Peter Fenelon Collier, 1898.

"Wörth" Franco-Prussian War.com

---. "Zur Orientierung über die Französische Armeelbid", qtd. in *The Mitrailleuse*, Military History Online. January 29, 2006.

Free Books by Charles River Editors

We have brand new titles available for free most days of the week. To see which of our titles are currently free, click on this link.

Discounted Books by Charles River Editors

We have titles at a discount price of just 99 cents everyday. To see which of our titles are currently 99 cents, click on this link.

Made in United States
North Haven, CT
25 March 2023

34550409R00039